"Reading Manda's book is much like being Manda's friend: she invites you in and tells the whole truth, and you feel welcomed, seen, and changed. *Soul Care to Save Your Life* lives up to everything it promises and more."

Annie F. Downs, *New York Times* bestselling author
of *That Sounds Fun*

"This book is a breath of fresh air for anyone and everyone who is suffocating beneath the weight of private struggles with sin. Manda's transparency and willingness to deal with what we prefer to keep hidden is a gift. Freedom lives within these pages."

Nona Jones, business executive, international speaker,
and bestselling author of *Success from the Inside Out*

"*Soul Care to Save Your Life* is both raw and practical. The personal stories Manda shares are equal parts uncomfortable and refreshingly honest. I found myself connecting to her stories and looking forward to the soul care practices throughout. Anyone who is ready for a future that looks different from your past will find this book catalytic and relevant."

Tim Stevens, executive pastor, Willow Creek Community Church

"Somehow, Manda has written a book that is essentially about confession—the ancient Christian practice of being fully known by God and others—in the most fresh, liberating, and page-turning manner. I cannot recommend this book enough but with one wink of a caution: this is not just a book that you read but a book that reads you."

Sharon Hodde Miller, author of *Nice*

"There's a chapter in this book titled 'Recipe for a Life Well Lived.' Honestly, that's what this entire book will be for you. A recipe to hold tight. A balm for the heavy parts of you. A manual toward a better version of yourself—one that practices soul care while keeping Jesus at the center of it all. This book is every bit as practical as it is prayer-filled, penned by someone who engages in the practice over the preaching. Get ready to be changed by the words in this book."

Hannah Brencher, author and TED Talk speaker

"In a world telling us we can find healing all by ourselves, my sister Manda Carpenter offers a refreshing alternative: the answer is in the daily downward and self-dying way of the cross. Through refreshingly honest storytelling, she offers us equally refreshing hope. *Soul Care to Save Your Life* is a devotional life raft that invites us to lean on the trustworthy truth of God, to heal, and to be transformed together."

Ashlee Eiland, colead pastor, Mars Hill Bible Church, and author of *Human(Kind)*

"Manda Carpenter courageously models how to bare our hearts in broad daylight and helps pave the way to freedom. Hold on to this one with both hands as you step out of hiding and reclaim the wholeness that awaits."

Shannan Martin, author of *Start with Hello, The Ministry of Ordinary Places,* and *Falling Free*

"Read this book slowly and with a highlighter. Manda delivers giant truths in gentle ways. Never before have I read a book that offered such incredible vulnerability while mapping out practical steps forward. Do you want meaningful relationships, increased peace, and an abundance of freedom? Then read this book now."

Anjuli Paschall, author of *Awake*

"Manda's words are raw and honest, taking us into the most unseen parts of her—yet she doesn't leave us there. Her heart turns to invite us into a life of more radical honesty, all while guiding us toward the healing our souls truly need."

Jena Holliday, artist, author, and founder of Spoonful of Faith

"Manda's unvarnished truth is not only refreshing but empowering. *Soul Care to Save Your Life* shows us that rather than hiding and denying even the most complex parts of ourselves, we can embrace the good, bad, and ugly. This is the path to healing, and on this essential journey of caring for ourselves and loving those around us well, her words constantly beckon us to remember that our light still shines even through what we may see as our own darkness."

Patricia A. Taylor, writer, anti-racism educator, and podcaster

"With vulnerability and approachability, Manda bravely goes first, showing us strength comes in naming our weaknesses. By weaving in her own struggles with actionable soul care steps, she gives us all permission to be in-process. She invites us not only to identify our wounds but to heal from them too. What a gift."

Kayla Craig, author of *To Light Their Way*

"If you know Manda, this is exactly the book you would expect—brave, honest, useful, and hopeful. But in a world filled with religious performances and half-truths, her book stands out even more. I've had the privilege of seeing firsthand the integrity between the story Manda tells and the life she lives, and I can't wait for readers to experience the same impact. Be careful picking it up—you won't be the same when you're done reading it."

Jason Adam Miller, founder and pastor, South Bend City Church

"*Soul Care to Save Your Life* is an invitation to pursue God, healing, spiritual growth, and emotional wellness. If you are looking for a vulnerable yet powerful book to start your soul care journey grounded in faith, Carpenter's book is for you."

Terence Lester, founder of Love Beyond Walls and author of *When We Stand*

"Manda Carpenter has a raw and rare gift to cut through all the chaos and confusion in life and take people to the place that matters most—their soul. Manda is a dear and treasured friend, and I have had the privilege of watching her live out these brave and beautiful words in her life. This book is more than just a gift; it will help you live a full and flourishing life."

Jeanne Stevens, founding lead pastor, Soul City Church, and author of *What's Here Now?*

"The subtitle of Manda Carpenter's new book says it all: radical honesty leads to real healing—and Manda proves it. With refreshing candor and remarkable insight, she shares her own hard-earned lessons of brokenness and healing while guiding readers along their own unique soul care journey. I didn't realize how much I needed this book. No matter what your story is, I think you'll discover the same is true for you."

Becky Keife, author of *The Simple Difference* and *No Better Mom for the Job*

"Manda has started a revolution of bravery with *Soul Care to Save Your Life*. She's ripped the Band-Aid off of shame, shone a light on hidden places, and called us all to lives of radical honesty and healing. And not only has she modeled it in this beautiful book but she's given us the practical tools to do the same. A must-read for your healing journey."

Toni J Collier, founder of Broken Crayons Still Color, author, and hope coach

"Amanda is a beautiful storyteller with a gift of vulnerability and honesty. Her powerful stories and authenticity give the reader permission to step into their own ring of radical honesty and uncover deep roots that need both exposure and tender love. Multiple times I found myself in tears, facing the hidden secrets I was still keeping that needed healing. Thank you for this glorious, healing treasure."

Kait Warman, bestselling author, dating coach, and founder of Heart of Dating

"Manda tells her truth in a way that encourages you to share your own just as deeply and openly. She makes words like *honesty*, *raw*, and *truth* positive in a world that considers them uncomfortable, scary, or overly trendy. *Soul Care to Save Your Life* does more than save your life. It gives life, hope, peace, and balance to living in your own truth."

Tanorria Askew, creative entrepreneur and author of *Staples + 5*

"I am incredibly grateful to God to not only know Manda as a friend but to see her live out what she has written here. This book is just like Manda: honest, hopeful, and helpful. What she offers is not only soul care to save a life but to shape it and form it and transform it into fullness and wholeness in Christ. I simply could not be prouder of my friend and could not be more excited for this book to finally be in your hands!"

Jarrett Stevens, colead pastor of Soul City Church and author of *Praying Through*

SOUL CARE
TO SAVE
YOUR LIFE

SOUL CARE
TO SAVE
YOUR LIFE

HOW RADICAL HONESTY
LEADS TO REAL HEALING

MANDA CARPENTER

BakerBooks

a division of Baker Publishing Group
Grand Rapids, Michigan

© 2022 by Manda Carpenter

Published by Baker Books
a division of Baker Publishing Group
PO Box 6287, Grand Rapids, MI 49516-6287
www.bakerbooks.com

Printed in the United States of America

Library of Congress Cataloging-in-Publication Data
Names: Carpenter, Manda, 1991– author.
Title: Soul care to save your life : how radical honesty leads to real healing / Manda Carpenter.
Description: Grand Rapids, MI : Baker Books, a division of Baker Publishing Group, [2022] | Includes bibliographical references.
Identifiers: LCCN 2021061094 | ISBN 9781540902139 (paperback) | ISBN 9781540902191 (casebound) | ISBN 9781493437436 (ebook)
Subjects: LCSH: Integrity–Religious aspects—Christianity. | Honesty. | Spiritual life—Christianity. | Christian life.
Classification: LCC BV4647.I55 C37 2022 | DDC 241/.4—dc23/eng/20220203
LC record available at https://lccn.loc.gov/2021061094

The names and details of the people and situations described in this book have been changed or presented in composite form in order to ensure the privacy of those with whom the author has worked.

Published in association with Illuminate Literary Agency, www.illuminateliterary.com

Baker Publishing Group publications use paper produced from sustainable forestry practices and post-consumer waste whenever possible.

22 23 24 25 26 27 28   7 6 5 4 3 2 1

My husband, E—your ongoing grace, wisdom, and longing for a better world are the reasons this book exists. Thank you for encouraging me to heal so I never have to hide.

Contents

Foreword by Morgan Harper Nichols   13

1. My Hidden Secret   15
   Soul Care Practice No. 1: Identify your hidden secrets.
2. Coming Clean   29
   Soul Care Practice No. 2: Develop a habit of confession.
3. What's *Really* Going On   47
   Soul Care Practice No. 3: Dig a layer deeper to find the root.
4. The One Thing That Changes Everything   59
   Soul Care Practice No. 4: Give and receive grace generously.
5. You Are Not the Only One   75
   Soul Care Practice No. 5: Embrace embarrassment for the sake of freedom.
6. Impressing Is Exhausting   87
   Soul Care Practice No. 6: Live in a rhythm of real.
7. You Are *Already* Good   105
   Soul Care Practice No. 7: Ground yourself in the good.
8. Autopilot   117
   Soul Care Practice No. 8: Exercise mindfulness.

9. All the Things We Cannot See   129
Soul Care Practice No. 9: Invest in your unseen self.

10. It's Not Them, It's You   141
Soul Care Practice No. 10: Take ownership consistently.

11. What Dreams Are Made Of   153
Soul Care Practice No. 11: Create sustainable rhythms.

12. The Question You Should Be Asking   165
Soul Care Practice No. 12: Recognize what you leave in your wake.

13. Recipe for a Life Well Lived   177
Soul Care Practice No. 13: Become insatiably curious.

14. Growth Doesn't Happen by Accident   191
Soul Care Practice No. 14: Match your will with your want.

15. Turn the Lights On   199
Soul Care Practice No. 15: Stay in the light.

Acknowledgments   213
Notes   217
About the Author   219

Foreword

Morgan Harper Nichols

I first met Manda a few years ago when she and I were both speaking at an event in Austin, Texas. I had never been much of a "speaker" up until that point, and in my true introverted nature, I was nervous. I'd spent months preparing an entire talk only to walk in the door and question it all. Who was I to say anything? What could anyone gather from my unfinished story? Over the past few years, I had managed to be present on the internet and connect with people by creating poetry and art. I was so grateful for the opportunity to do this work, but the real world felt a lot messier. I was a struggling freelancer. I was in the last year of my twenties, trying to figure out what I was going to do with my life. I didn't feel ready to speak yet. In my mind, I had a lot more work to do first.

The event began, and my overthinking continued. As I struggled to quiet the inner chatter, Manda's presence broke through the noise in my mind. When she took the stage and shared her story, everyone in the room received an invitation to pay attention to the beauty and power of transformation.

As Manda shared her highs, her lows, and the ways she was continuing to grow, I reflected on my own journey. A journey that was, very much so, still in process . . . exactly how it was meant to be. I took a deep breath, and this truth rose up from the depths of my soul: *OK, we're all still learning here. I'll speak about what I've learned and what I'm still learning. That's all I need to do.*

I walked away from that event a little less afraid to share my story as-is. I also walked away with a newfound friend in Manda. Since then, we have been able to swap stories and share ideas that remind me it's a beautiful thing to learn as we go. Healing happens on the path. Soul work happens in the day-to-day.

In this book, you will encounter the words of a woman who is doing the work and is inviting you to journey with her. Take a deep breath and get ready to grow in your awareness of the full landscape of your life. Get ready to travel through the desert, to the sea, and all of the places in between, knowing that in the well of your soul, you are whole. You are still becoming who you were made to be.

CHAPTER 1

My Hidden Secret

My husband, Eric, and I are city people through and through. All of our kids have been born and raised in the city too. So when we took our three big boys camping for the first time, it was an unforgettable experience, to say the least.

One year into our marriage, we left the comfort of small-town Indiana, where our family and friends lived right around the corner, to set out on an adventure. We landed in Chicago and unexpectedly stayed for five years. Now, Los Angeles, the city we used to frequent for beach getaways and creative energy, is our home. We gravitate toward big cities because we enjoy being immersed in a diverse population, having access to public transportation, and avoiding yard work. Everyone used to tease us about moving to the burbs once we had kids, but we chose our own path. We made a conscious decision not to have biological children for the first five years of our marriage and instead became parents through foster care.

We have had over fifteen children in our care throughout our foster parenting journey. In early 2021, I gave birth to our first biological child, but when I initially set out to write this book, we had three boys living under our roof: Goof, age thirteen; Bear, age nine; and Skittles, age six. Those aren't their legal names, of course, but rather their chosen nicknames. It's a crazy thing to consider, but if we hadn't chosen to live in Chicago, we would never have received the call to care for them. Like every child I've ever potty-trained or taught how to write their name, these boys came into my home total strangers and left as part of my family forever. And as all children do, they have each been used by God to chip away at my pride, magnify my selfishness, and test my patience. They give me the best seat in the house of grace, joy, and resilience.

Our urban lifestyle has increased our proximity to diversity and our awareness of needs we were blissfully ignorant of in the small towns we grew up in. Chicago and Los Angeles have grown and stretched us until, over time, we are no longer who we once were—a beautiful and rare gift in a world where many seem to forget that growth doesn't have to end with puberty. Chicago taught me many things, but none top the belief that there isn't a single person we wouldn't love if we knew their story. Given proximity and enough time, knowledge and empathy will almost always replace judgment and ignorance. After a while, we fit in so well living in the concrete jungle that you'd never know we weren't native to it. But it makes us appreciate the times we get away and are surrounded by nature even more.

Unawareness Hurts

When we took our big boys camping, it was every bit as dirty, fun, and fattening as I'd hoped it would be. One of my proudest moments was when the younger two chose to poop in the woods rather than walk a short distance to the public restrooms near our campsite. These city kids didn't need any help embracing the wilderness. The first evening, they couldn't wait to make s'mores. An avid lover of all things chocolate and sweet, I did not object. Out came the roasting sticks, marshmallows, chocolate, graham crackers—and my anxiety, as I prayed no one would accidentally set themselves on fire.

With gentle safety reminders here and there—"Yes, your cotton sweatshirt will catch fire if you touch it with a marshmallow that's on fire!"—everything was going great, and the boys were having a blast. I'm pretty sure they ate four large s'mores each.

Here we were: an unlikely family made up of different DNA, skin colors, and preferences with so much love and laughter that no one would guess we'd only known each other for nine months. If the world were as it should be, there wouldn't be a need for foster care. The thought brings joy to my soul. Still, there are moments in our journey where everything is beautiful in its own way, and I think, *We could've missed this.* It's what keeps us saying yes to partnering with families in crisis. Until heaven comes down and there is no poverty, no unhealed trauma, and accessible help for everyone, there will be a need for foster care. It's all I think about when I lay my head down at night. So, I embrace that I am not God, I cannot save the world, and I too need saving. And I simply keep saying, "Yes, we'll make room."

There we were, sitting around the campfire peacefully, until Bear and Skittles began poking the burning logs with their roasting sticks, creating unnecessary clouds of ash and smoke. Their playing around notoriously turns into play fighting, so I warned them to be careful (mommin' at its finest). Soon the sun painted the sky with gorgeous hues of red, orange, and pink. Our boys called their mom to say goodnight, a part of our nightly routine few families can relate with. They were in awe as their mom told them about the sky from her view. Despite distance and everything else that separated them from her, our boys realized that no matter how much time passed between visits and calls, they could always look up and know she also lived under the same sky. Children shouldn't have to find comfort in these things, but sometimes it's the best we can offer. After they hung up, the hues faded to black, and we could soon only see each other's faces in the glowing firelight.

Because it never rains until you're camping with three kids, the air began to shift, and a downpour began to brew. What started as a light drizzle quickly turned into a tsunami. (OK, I'm a little dramatic, but you get the point.) Eric grabbed a flashlight and coached us on what to grab and where to go. I set out to protect our hot dog buns and other dry food by gathering it all up to put it in the back of our vehicle. In the middle of all this hustle and bustle, I felt a burning hot roasting stick jab my lower leg.

I screamed, and a few linguistically colorful words came out of my mouth. Eric ran over with his flashlight, shining a light on my bloody wound. My face was covered in tears masked by the pouring rain. At the sight of my injury, the kids froze. Bear dropped his stick and began bawling. He screamed, "I didn't mean to! I didn't mean to!" at the top of his lungs.

Multitasking as parents learn to do so well, Eric helped calmed our tender child, whose past trauma made him believe he was going to be harmed by accidentally causing this incident, while tending to me too. His flashlight revealed two big holes in my pants where the stick had burned right through the material. Just below the kneecap, I'd been branded. It felt about as bad as it looked.

I hobbled over to the picnic table, taking a moment to catch my breath and keeping my leg straight. Almost as if God saw our struggles and commanded the rain to cease, it died off. Eric turned on our vehicle headlights so everyone could see better. I called Bear over. "You are not in trouble, baby," I told him. "It's OK. I'm all right. You're not in trouble. Accidents happen. I know you weren't trying to hurt me." I put my arms around him, and he nuzzled up to my chest, sobbing with relief.

When the rain came down, Bear had reacted like we all did and hopped out of his seat. Unfortunately, he didn't set down his hot roasting stick. He wasn't thinking about how dangerous it was to run with a sharp, scalding hot object. An hour prior, there had been a couple of close calls with his older brother's eyeballs; now my leg had been branded, all because of a lack of awareness.

(I'm happy to report that my leg is completely healed, and Bear recovered emotionally.)

At nearly 3:00 a.m., I lay awake in the tent, relieved that everyone else was sound asleep and replaying the best parts of the day in my mind. In that time of reflection, I experienced a moment of enlightenment and jotted myself a note:

> When we lack awareness and stumble around in the dark, we aren't only putting ourselves in danger but burn other people and then have to deal with the aftermath of feeling ashamed.

I was reminded by my sweet boy, Bear, that when we choose to live unaware and in the dark, we aren't only hurting ourselves; we hurt other people in the process.

Unawareness Costs Us

I know what it's like to hurt people because of my own unawareness. One decade ago, I lost a few friends and the respect of an entire family after making a huge mistake that can be traced back to my lack of maturity, integrity—and ultimately, inner awareness.

At the time, I had just gotten out of a longstanding relationship with my college boyfriend. We were trying to stay friends—a tactic I don't recommend. He reached out to me to share some very private and personal news about his family, asking me for my word that I would not tell anyone. He shared that his younger sister, whom I had grown to be friends with, was pregnant. The pregnancy wasn't planned, and she was not married. Sadly, this was a huge opportunity for gossip in a small town with conservative Christian roots.

My ex-boyfriend didn't say anything negative; he simply wanted to tell me the news because he was shocked. Up until a few weeks prior, I had been the person he shared these kinds of intimate life details with. Even though his sister was someone I cared deeply

19

about, I didn't pause to consider my responsibility, my commitment to maintain discretion, or her feelings. Instead, I took this sensitive information and shared it with some of our mutual friends. I want to believe that my intention wasn't to gossip, but that's precisely what I did. Not only did I disregard my promise to hold this sensitive information wisely but I went out of my way to disperse it—via text messages, and including my judgmental thoughts about the whole thing. Word got back to her, as gossip tends to, and she reached out to me. She was hurt and disgusted. I'd made a huge mistake. Why had I been so cruel? I will never forget the feeling of longing to take it all back at that moment. That mistake became a lifelong lesson.

Have you ever made a mistake so dumb that you wish you could go back in time and have a do-over? You replay the incident over and over again, but it doesn't change reality. What's done is done. We can't go back in time to fix our lowest, ugliest moments, but we can learn from them.

What that situation revealed to me was that I had a gossip problem. I learned I would go to great, stupid lengths to connect with my friends—even though talking about other people isn't what true friendship is built on. I also learned I had some self-righteous tendencies and a bad habit of judging others that needed to be addressed. I wasn't aware of these things until it all hit the fan and I was left to clean up the mess.

Imagine if I could have avoided the pain of it all. The pain of having people I care about angry with me, the pain of beating myself up over it, and especially the pain I caused a young woman in the midst of her unexpected pregnancy. What if instead I had been in tune with myself to the point where I chose to journal my thoughts about this sensitive information before sending any texts? Perhaps I could have called her up to have a conversation or scheduled a therapy session to figure out why something that had nothing to do with me caused such a big reaction inside me. But I didn't, because I wasn't living in that state of consciousness.

Unawareness causes unnecessary pain in our lives and in the lives of people we love. This particular incident cost me my reputation, respect, and relationships. The most painful cost of all was the loss of friendship. Since then, no amount of time or apology letters I've written have been able to mend the hurt or restore what I wrecked. We cannot always control if we get a happy ending, but we can control if we learn as we move forward.

Awareness Creates a Sacred Opportunity

Self-awareness at a soul level is vital if we want to live healthy and deeply meaningful lives that evolve. I don't want to be the same person twenty-five years from now. I don't want to lose friends or family members because I neglected to do the inner work. I want to thrive, grow, and learn. I want to be more like Jesus and embody the fruits of the Holy Spirit without striving or focusing on behavior modification.

While working at a church a few years ago, I met a woman, Rocio, who would become my mentor—someone I hoped would help me grow in self-awareness. At the time, Rocio was the assistant to our lead pastor's office, and I was the first impressions director. I never had a hard time making a great first impression, but always believed if people really knew me—all of me—they wouldn't think I was so great after all. *Oh, the irony.* Our jobs didn't lead us to interact with each other a whole bunch, but we crossed paths enough for me to notice she carried herself with such grace and poise. Whenever I had a conversation with her, I felt like I'd just cozied up next to my grandmother on the sofa with a box of chocolates. It was so comfortable and easy. Though she's nowhere near old enough to be my grandmother or even my mother, this kind and beautiful Latina woman, who stands five inches shorter than me, embodied empathy, and in her presence I felt safe.

As a staff team, we have a birthday tradition of gathering around a long table to share a word with the person whose birthday we are celebrating. The word can be an affirmation of who they are or a word of encouragement for them in the coming year. We always assign one person to record every word shared so the birthday guy or gal can have it as a keepsake.

I had only been on the team for two months when September, my birthday month, rolled around, and it was my turn to be celebrated at that table. Everyone looked me in the eyes and shared a word for me that felt genuine and inspiring even though they didn't know me super well. Although everyone said really kind and affirming things about me, Rocio's words were different and caught my attention.

"It has been a joy getting to know you. My word for you was going to be *kind* because you are genuinely kind, but instead my word for you is where I feel like God is leading you next. It's *home* and it's also *owner*. Maybe it's home-dash-owner, but I want you to write it down home-slash-owner," she instructed the scribe.

home-owner

home/owner

At the time, this didn't have any real significance to me. Rocio and I didn't know each other very well yet, but as time went on, I consistently felt seen and understood by her. As someone who identifies as an Enneagram 8 (see chapter 6), I found this to be huge. She became such a safe relationship for me, and I felt free to be myself. You know the type of person you don't have to second-guess your words around, the type who gives you confidence they have your back without ever saying a word? That's Rocio. This ultimately led me to ask her to be my mentor.

"Hey! I feel weird asking you this, but . . . would you, um, maybe want to be my mentor?" I stumbled over my words, nervous of being rejected and feeling like an idiot. I added, "I know you're busy with work and being a mom and wife and all, so I just want you to know I'm not super needy . . . I don't need a lot of your time. Really. I just think maybe it would be cool to learn from you."

Her eyes smiled at me.

"It's just when I think about who I feel like really *gets* me, it's you," I added. "And I admire you for so many reasons. Plus, don't you do some mentor stuff like this for others—"

She cut me off before I could ramble any longer. "I would be honored," she said. It was as if she had been waiting for this moment, for me to ask her or be ready. Something about it felt divine.

Our mentorship began with her asking me what kind of things I wanted to tackle and grow in. I didn't have clarity, so I simply expressed my desire to be a better follower of Jesus, wife, and writer. We began by meeting weekly for lunch, and our relationship evolved organically to daily texts and spontaneous phone calls. God was up to something through our mentorship, even though neither of us knew for sure what it was.

Awareness Cultivates Hope

I had never acknowledged my obsession with male attention because I wasn't aware enough to realize that's what it was. That is, until the day it hit me square in the face as I hit the cold, hard floor of rock bottom.

When I first began dating Eric, my subconscious but very real need for a male to desire me felt fulfilled. However, soon enough our married life felt "normal," and I reentered the unspoken struggle I had been tempted by throughout my entire life.

My eyes and mind began to wander. I found it increasingly difficult to resist males who showed me attention. What would start as a harmless compliment left me longing for more. I wanted to be desired, and it was especially tempting to feel desired by someone other than my husband if things with him were in a rough spot—say, when he got busy with work and I felt like an afterthought. During our first year of marriage this happened on random occasions, such as when a handsome stranger in a coffee shop struck up a conversation with me and complimented my eyes. I felt desired and found fulfillment. *My husband didn't tell me I looked beautiful this morning, and it's not my fault this other guy did*, I told myself as I justified my flirty behavior. I wasn't doing anything wrong by feeling attractive and desired by other guys, so long as I didn't act on it. Over time, though, my excuses and justifying increased, and my boundary lines got blurry.

No one wakes up one day and says, "Today is the day I'm going to have an affair," or "Today is the day I'm going to become addicted to pornography." People don't just decide, "Today is the day I'm going to become an alcoholic," or "Today is the day I'm going to rack up a ton of credit card debt." These addictions happen as, over time, a person remains unaware of their shadow side and temptations. This is often why people, like me, get to some sort of crisis moment and think, *How in the world did I get here?* We can't believe it, and yet, from an outsider's perspective, it's usually clear as daylight.

One day I committed what I believed was the unforgiveable sin of infidelity. I allowed one man to cross the much-needed-but-seriously-lacking boundary lines in my life. He probably knew what he was doing all along, but I did not. I wasn't aware until it was too late—and that's precisely the problem.

I couldn't believe what happened, but as I retraced my steps it was so obvious—which made me feel even more ashamed. There were no excuses or ways to justify it. My unawareness of the sin I was entangled in led me to make the biggest mistake of my life. All along were red flags I'd ignored, and had I been living consciously they could have served as major stop signs. Things such as:

- How often he complimented me.
- How much I enjoyed his attention.
- How often he communicated with me despite knowing I was married.

- How I hid certain things about him and our friendship from my husband.
- How he gave me gifts and crossed the line on what an appropriate friendship looks like between two heterosexual people of the opposite sex.
- How I went out of my way to make him happy.
- The overall amount of time and energy both he and I invested in each other.

All of it was inappropriate. None of it was "no big deal" as I had been telling myself all along. I'm now convinced there is no such thing as harmless flirting when you are married. I now hold the belief that if we have to hide something from our spouse, it's wrong—period. No ifs, ands, or buts about it.

In the aftermath of what occurred, I promised myself to never be so ignorant and heedless ever again. I was finally aware of my shadow side—because I saw the shadow once the light poured in: I was addicted to affirmation from men. I started going to individual counseling and brought this new self-knowledge to my counselor. However, I did not tell her (or anyone) about the event that had taken place and had ultimately awakened me to this awareness. I thought it was a secret I would take to my grave.

While it's great I had become conscious of my struggle and started therapy, the secrecy of my mistake left me feeling isolated and ashamed. Day by day I looked up, hoping to see the light, but it was as if the lid was closing and less light was pouring in. Some days the lid was propped open just enough to let a little light in—but on those days, it rained. It rained so hard it poured, and the water was inching up to my shoulders. As the water rose, so did my anxiety. There were no good days. I grew extremely depressed.

God's Spirit had been whispering to me, telling me to go to my husband and get this off my chest. To tell the truth. Then I would be free from the guilt I was carrying. The Enemy had also been whispering, convincing me that I was damaged and had ruined my life. I wrestled with them both for over a year. Most days, I felt like I was drowning. I couldn't go more than a few hours without thinking about my addiction, what had happened, and how terrified I was of anyone finding out.

Occasionally thoughts of sitting down and spilling the tea would come. I'd get a burst of energy, thinking *Today's the day I'm finally going to confess.* But just as quickly as those bursts jolted through my body, the lies of the Enemy came storming around me like a colony of bees. The buzzing was so loud and the culpability so real. I was desperate to make it stop. This was a matter of truth or death. I came to a decision: trust God or end my life.

When you truly believe the world will come crashing down if anyone finds out something about you, it's terrifying. Every day is filled with fear and shame. Sometimes intrusive thoughts enter your mind, and you imagine vanishing from the earth so you can be free of it all. My depression took me to low valleys I didn't think were possible. I've met women who have gone through something eerily similar after having an abortion. I've met both men and women who tell me this was their experience while silently battling a porn addiction. I have friends in the LGBTQ+ community who tell me they contemplated suicide before coming out because they truly believed it would be worse for them to face rejection from people they love than to embrace their true identity. Being honest about your sexuality is vastly different from doing something you know is wrong—like I did—but the depression many people, especially conservative Christians, experience is similar. It's no wonder an LGBTQ+ person seriously contemplates suicide at almost three times the rate of someone who is heterosexual.[1]

As I contemplated ending my life, I thought, *What if I tell Rocio? If she offers me hope, I can get through this. If I tell her and she reacts the way I think she and everyone else will react, I am better off dead.* After all, Rocio was heaven-sent.

My guess is that you have sin or a secret struggle in your life only you know exists. It might feel small in comparison to mine, or maybe you've written a story that yours is even worse. Maybe it's recurring, or perhaps you've tried to cover it up in fear of what someone might think if they knew. And you would do just about anything to be cured of it.

The Enemy might, at some point in time, try to convince you that the only cure is to end your life. I want you to hear me: **this is a ploy.** He comes to steal, kill, and destroy. Don't buy it. God can heal and restore you—and he will if you give him the chance. There is no magic cure to overcoming your demons or greatest temptations. There is no self-help book with ten steps to conquering your innermost battles. There is nothing that can fill the void in your soul forever or sustain transformation other than Jesus.

If I'm honest, I never used to believe in prophecy or what I considered to be all that crazy, weird spiritual stuff, but now I do. I do because Rocio's birthday word for me came to fruition. I didn't go home to be with Jesus. I came back home to him here on earth. And it all happened because I owned my sin rather than trying to hide it.

For you were once darkness, but now you are light in the Lord. Live as children of light (for the fruit of the light consists in all goodness, righteousness and truth) and find out what pleases the Lord. Have nothing to do with the fruitless deeds of darkness, but rather expose them. It is shameful even to mention what the disobedient do in secret. But everything exposed by the light becomes visible—and everything that is illuminated becomes a light. This is why it is said:

"Wake up, sleeper,
rise from the dead,
and Christ will shine on you." (Eph. 5:8–14)

SOUL CARE PRACTICE NO. 1

Identify your hidden secrets.

Be Radically Honest with Yourself

1. What do you feel shame about?
2. Which struggle shows up repeatedly in your relationships?
3. When are you most tempted to lie, cover up, or hide?
4. Imagine a healthy, healed version of yourself—how is it different from you right now?
5. Why did you pick up this book?

CHAPTER 2

Coming Clean

I'd texted Rocio the details of where to meet me, and she walked into a glass-enclosed area of our church known as the gallery, where I was seated. I was already feeling nervous and overly exposed, even though I had yet to bare my soul. The shiny, glass walls didn't provide any real comfort, but it was the only quiet, unoccupied space where I could be certain no one would overhear our conversation, so I made it work.

"Hey, love," she said in a curious tone as she walked in, embracing me for an extra-long hug. "This is unusual. What's going on?" She looked puzzled.

Rocio and I met regularly, and this was not our normal time. It was the middle of a Tuesday afternoon. I was supposed to be working, but this was urgent. I'd made the decision to choose truth over death. I decided to take God at his word when he said there would be grace waiting for me.

As if my unwashed hair and the awfully dark circles beneath my eyes didn't give it away, I began by telling her my doctor had diagnosed me with depression. Then I let her know I'd been struggling to get out of bed in the mornings. I had been covering up how awful I looked with makeup and baseball caps, but the truth was that I was not well. I felt ugly, and not just on the outside. It didn't help that I wasn't taking care of myself physically, emotionally, or spiritually. I showed her the prescription my doctor had started me on. She listened and nodded. In between sentences I blew my nose and caught my breath. Tears were streaming, and I couldn't seem to pull myself together. When Rocio tried to comfort me, I felt even more embarrassed and ashamed, because little did she know that it wasn't the diagnosis of depression upsetting me but rather the situation that had led me to this dark place. I was an emotional wreck, full of anxiety and fear. I needed to confess this secret I'd been carrying for so long. I'm pretty sure I gave forty-seven prefaces and disclaimers before I finally got it out.

In the least eloquent way, I blurted, "I made a huge mistake several years ago before I started working here at the church. I was unfaithful to Eric early in our marriage, and I've kept it a secret. It has been eating me alive. It won't leave my conscious mind and, to be honest, I can't see a way out of this other than being gone."

Rocio didn't flinch. She didn't gasp or say what I felt: that I'd been living a lie. She locked eyes with me and told me I was safe. She didn't ask for details or coax me into sharing more. She sat there and held space for me to get this confession off my chest. More importantly, she left room for the Spirit to reveal that I was not better off dead.

Maya Angelou reportedly once said, "I've learned that people will forget what you said, people will forget what you did, but people will never forget how you made them feel."[1] It's true. I don't recall what Rocio's exact words were in response to my confession, and I only vaguely remember feeling her hand on mine. What's vivid years later is how she made me feel: hopeful.

She didn't meet me with shame. She didn't get angry or express her disappointment. She knew I was human and capable of sin; therefore, the shock I'd anticipated never appeared. She didn't give me false hope that there wouldn't be any consequences. She simply listened. She stayed put. She asked questions to help me process and made sure I wasn't still contemplating suicide. She watched as I scheduled an emergency appointment to see my counselor before the week ended and offered concrete next steps so that I could make this confession to the person I needed to most: my husband. I felt relief rush through my veins. Rocio never promised he would stay with me or forgive me, but by her response, she made me realize that no matter what happened, I was still a woman with breath in her lungs and a beating heart. So, no matter how things played out, God was not done with me. She gave me every reason to live simply by staying with me.

Shattering Shame

Here I was—fully known and fully loved. How could it be? No longer would those words roll off my tongue or be sung aloud from my lips nonchalantly. They held real meaning now, the kind of meaning that could knock me off my feet and heal my deepest voids. The kind of meaning that would change the entire trajectory of my life. This, I know, is the definition of grace: undeserved, unfathomable, and liberating.

Newly unshackled and lighter than I'd felt in many months, I raced home to my husband. The fear of losing him was still terrifying but no longer paralyzing. I was eager to give him what he deserved all along: the truth.

I came through our apartment door a hot mess with a red nose, tearstained cheeks, and massive sweat stains extending far beyond my armpits. I asked him to sit down and assured him that no one had died—because he began panicking, as any person would at the sight of me in that moment.

My sentences all bled together as I apologized profusely, confessed what I had done, and assured him that I took full responsibility for my actions. I'll never forget the look of complete shock on his face. I'll never forget how terrible I felt watching as he coiled up on the couch and sobbed. I'll never forget all of the conversations we had that evening and in the days that followed.

I'll also never forget that the very first words out of his mouth were, "I still love you."

Out of all the things he could have said in response, this was nowhere in my realm of expectation. *You're kidding me, right?* When he could've said, "How could you?" or "I hate you!" he reminded me that he loved me. His very first words aligned with God's words—the truth and grace that had been pulling me toward the light in this tug-of-war for my soul.

Eric didn't make any promises or instantly assure me we would get through this. He was slow to speak and, even in his anger, remained levelheaded.

Time, new boundaries, accountability, mentors, and counseling helped us on the path to healing when it could've been easier for him to throw in the towel on our marriage. I have no doubt that his initial response to my confession and his wisdom in the days that followed are primary reasons we were able to heal and recover from this brokenness.

I'd be lying if I said there weren't moments after I made my confession when I wondered if I'd made a terrible mistake in sharing a secret that very well could have remained hidden. *Couldn't I have just kept it to myself? It's not like it was ongoing. Didn't I hurt Eric even more by sharing about something that took place so long ago? I get that I risked losing my marriage when I made that mistake, but now I've really put my marriage in a bind.*

Years later, knowing all that I know now, I am confident that *even if* I had somehow managed to keep my secret buried inside without it causing me to end my life, I would have never been able to experience healing for myself—not just in my marriage—and that is the most devastating ending I can think of. Healing isn't just about not having to hide a secret, an isolated incident, or a habit you're ashamed of, though that freedom cannot be undervalued.

Healing is a necessary step in the path to living whole and pursuing a life that has great purpose.

Radical honesty leads to real healing. Radical honesty is exactly that: radical. It's not just telling the truth when it's easy; it's about searching for the truth and going out of our way to dig up anything that is untrue.

The freedom found in leaving the dark to live in the light is what saved my life, saved my marriage, and led me to where I am now. It's an odd and quite frankly scary thing for me to look back and think I almost ended my life in fear that there would be no way out. I wake up every day to a life I love that's beyond my wildest imagination. A life that is honest and full of purpose and love.

Choosing Integrity

While I felt enormous weight lifted after admitting my sin, apologizing, and asking for forgiveness from my husband, my healing didn't happen in one fell swoop. It's been a pilgrimage, full of daily choices to stay in the light. I suspect I'll always need to remain vigilant. Maybe that sounds exhausting to you: living consciously and doing inner work to access radical honesty throughout your entire life. It's *not* easy. I don't want to undersell just how much work it actually is and how much courage it requires. But I can assure you, *impressing* is even more exhausting.

Impressing is going about your everyday life knowing that you aren't living with complete integrity. Impressing chooses to cover up and mask what's bubbling up beneath the surface. Impressing is existing without digging in deep because what you may encounter is weird, scary, or shameful. When I didn't choose integrity, covered things up, and avoided going deep, I was exhausted and imprisoned—far more drained than when I courageously chose radical honesty and now experience healing day after day.

For me, healing takes many different forms. It's an ongoing practice of confessing, implementing boundaries from a place of love (not fear) for myself and those I care deeply about, and choosing to believe I am more than the sum of my mistakes. For as long as I wake up with a beating heart and breath in my lungs, I have to believe that God has me here for a reason. I don't always feel clear about what that reason is, but maybe it's not one particular thing. Perhaps I'm alive simply to function from a deep belief that I'm good, loved, and chosen—and that what those beliefs produce in me is better than what any of my striving to prove myself or earn my identity could otherwise bring to the world. For years I've been in a wildly complex, multilayered healing process, but that's where I land over and over again.

Counseling and journaling have been helpful for different reasons, and inviting others into my weakness, especially my husband, has brought about so much restoration and deepened our intimacy more than ever before. As you continue reading, you'll get to know more about my healing and transformational journey, but right now I want you to consider this one question: What habit, addiction, or secret do you keep hidden that you need to get radically honest about in order to move toward healing?

Inner Awareness > Outward Appearances

One evening Eric flew in from a work trip, and I burst into laughter upon the sight of him. My sweet husband is notorious for misplacing or forgetting things—you could say he's not the most mindful person. This time, it wasn't a lost wallet (that one made me angry). It wasn't that he forgot his phone in the Uber (that one made me frantic). On this particular evening, he had no idea what I was laughing at.

"You do realize your shirt is on inside out, and you have an enormous stain on your pants, right?" I teased. He was clueless. He walked into our bedroom and stood in front of the long mirror.

"What? I'm a mess!" As he realized his shirt must have been like that during all of the day's meetings and presentations, he felt

34

super embarrassed. He contemplated what the food stain on his pants was and how long it might have been there. Was it the tacos at lunch or the chili cheese corn dog at the airport? He hoped for the latter. After acknowledging there was nothing he could do about the mishap, he laughed it off. I've always admired his ability to let things roll off his shoulders. He tossed his dirty laundry into the hamper and jumped in the shower. We chalked it up as another "Only Eric" story for the books. In the grand scheme of life, stained pants and an inside-out shirt only have the ramifications of temporary embarrassment . . . no one is at risk of getting hurt. When it comes to our outward appearances, awareness is helpful but not detrimental. But when it comes to what's going on internally, a lack of awareness holds much greater consequences.

Self-awareness is a conscious, accurate understanding of ourselves that requires our integrity, motives, and desires to be transparent. To become this self-aware, we have to face our own inner reality, which is both beautiful and terrifying.

Society places a greater emphasis on appearances because it's the easy part. Plus, we care so much about what people think of us. We're trained to focus on what's seen, because to many, that's all that matters. For others, it's too hard or scary or deep or vulnerable to look inward and deal with what's inside. This is precisely why so many people go through life and end up being the same person with the same beliefs making the same mistakes at the age of seventy-five as they did at twenty-five. It's also why we hurt ourselves and other people. When we lack inner awareness, the repercussions are brutal.

My husband, even with his inside-out shirt and food-stained pants, is more self-aware than I am in the areas that actually matter. He may not be aware of small, external things, but he is hyperaware of his integrity, motives, and desires. I picked up on this early in our dating days. He's radically honest. He doesn't say what he wishes were true, he says the truth. Even with small things that don't seem to matter, like saying, "I'll be there in ten minutes" if he's really going to be there in twenty. He won't go in the express checkout line designated for fifteen items or less if he has sixteen. To him, fudging the truth has always been a slippery slope, so he doesn't do it. I first admired this about him because I thought it was cute and quirky. After my own major setback, I gained a whole new appreciation for how seriously he takes integrity. It's as if we couldn't possibly take integrity too far—and I really respect anyone who tries to do so.

Eric has also never shied away from discussing topics most people want to avoid, like the things he struggles with. In fact, he was very open when we first discussed pornography. He expressed his personal views and admitted his struggles with it. He was self-aware enough to pinpoint when and why he ever returned to porn despite knowing it wasn't something he wanted to partake in. He took initiative to put accountability in place for himself, and I never had to ask him to do so.

Over a decade into our relationship, Eric is self-aware and radically honest enough to admit that sometimes he is tempted to withhold information from me. He knows how I'll likely react and wants to avoid a fight, whether it's a minor incident with one of our kids (like the time Goof lost hundreds of dollars raised for a school fundraiser, resulting in us having to fork over the funds ourselves) or when he wants to talk with me about how I could do a better job making space for others in conversation. Despite having good intentions for withholding information from me, he chooses instead to be forthcoming. This is the beautiful outcome of attending counseling together. We have learned to repair what we don't want to repeat. And instead of focusing on the fact that I'm upset when Eric doesn't tell me something, we focus on *why* he didn't want to tell me. Our counselor has taught us how to tackle the root, which ultimately leads us to greater awareness, deeper understanding, and more compassion toward ourselves and each other.

For the first three years of our marriage, our biggest recurring conflict happened whenever we were driving together. As a control freak, I've always had a hard time relaxing as a passenger when someone else is driving, but with Eric's speeding habit and easily distractible personality, I really struggled. I would point out every stop sign proactively, scream "Brake!" whenever I saw the red lights appear on the car in front of us, and repeatedly point out the speed limit. All of this really annoyed Eric. (Can you blame him? Also, am I the only wife who can't handle her husband's driving? Please send help in the form of group therapy.) While my behavior was probably . . . err, most definitely . . . caused by my irrational fears and subconscious need to be in control, I needed him to work with me instead of telling me to stop micromanaging his driving and reminding me that he had never been in an accident. We had to get below the surface and resolve this together so that it didn't recur every single time we were in the car. Though my nagging eventually wore him down, and Eric slowed down and drove like a grandpa, I'd gotten "what I wanted" but felt defeated and frustrated. He couldn't understand why I was so uptight over "nothing." I didn't know how to explain to him the depths of anxiety I had every time I was in a car driven by someone else. I'd never really spent time reflecting on it. I just thought it was the way I was.

When we finally brought this up with our counselor, she helped me get to the root of the issue. I became aware that my childhood wounds were a direct correlation. I remember feeling scared and out of control whenever I rode in the car with my dad because he drove like a madman with extreme road rage. It made sense to my counselor that whenever I sensed even a hint that someone wasn't being hyperaware of other drivers on the road, I felt that same fear and sense of instability arise. Now, anytime I feel this way, whether I'm in a vehicle or elsewhere, I tell Eric and he takes it seriously. He asks me questions and provides gentle support so that I can overcome the anxiety that once overpowered every rational part of me. Without ever going beyond the belief that I had "micromanaging tendencies" or discovering why I was so triggered by certain driving behaviors, our frequent car fights would undoubtedly have continued to take place until we drove each other absolutely insane.

I appreciate what one of my favorite authors, Peter Scazzero, says about people who lack inner awareness:

> They ignore emotion-related messages their body may send— fatigue, stress-induced illness, weight gain, ulcers, headaches, or depression. They avoid reflecting on their fears, sadness, or anger, and fail to consider how God might be trying to communicate with them through these "difficult" emotions. They struggle to articulate the reasons for their emotional triggers, their overreactions in the present rooted in difficult experiences from their past. They remain unaware of how issues from their family of origin have impacted who they are today. This lack of emotional awareness also extends to their personal and professional relationships. In fact, they are often blind to the emotional impact they have on others.[2]

Sure, you don't want to show up for a job interview or big presentation with your shirt turned inside out or food stains on your pants, but the stakes are much higher when you show up to your life with self-ignorance where self-knowledge belongs.

A lack of awareness that I seek affirmation from men could very well lead me down a dark, dangerous path of destruction. A lack of awareness that you play the victim in every situation could very well lead you to constant turnover in all of your relationships. A lack of awareness that you use food or alcohol for comfort could very well lead you on a path toward obesity or alcoholism. The examples I give might sound extreme, but they aren't. They are real issues many different people struggle with but don't know why, and they have no idea how to get out of their unhealthy cycle to experience real healing.

How to Become More Aware

Clay Scroggins, author of *How to Lead When You're Not in Charge*, once told me on a Skype call, "You can't know where you're going until you know where you already are." And it's true. We can't think about being "better," healing, or growing in certain areas until we have a clear starting point. He gave the example of a shopping mall directory. You know, the one that tells you where Auntie Anne's Pretzels is? He explained that the most important piece of the directory is actually the star that says, "You are here," because you can't get where you want to go until you know where you are.

Here are my favorite tools to pursue awareness.

1. Find a Trusted Mirror

The reality is, we can look in a mirror to get a real, honest picture of how things look on the outside, but it won't show us an honest picture of our souls. To see our souls and become aware of what's inside, we need a mirror that can't be bought at Target. However, one might be found in the church.

My mirror holders are my husband, my mentor, and a handful of friends I can count on to be wholly transparent with me. For some other people, I know it's their pastor, a therapist, or an older adult they admire and respect. Really, anyone who is emotionally intelligent and willing can be a mirror holder to help you see a true picture of your inner reflection. A good mirror holder does not tell you what you want to hear but rather what you need to hear. They ask questions to help you get out of the weeds and into the root and awaken you to your most conscious self. There's no prerequisite or list of standards; just look for someone who's healthy and exudes light.

My therapist and my mentor both knew the mistake I made in my marriage was not because I wasn't happy with Eric or because I was a chronic cheater. They both knew and helped me fully understand the root of my weeds. Both of these women were incredible mirror holders because they revealed a true reflection of myself, including the unseen wrestling that took place unconsciously within my soul. Truthfully, I would've much rather heard, "You made a mistake because you were twenty-four years old and immature," but that wasn't the *whole* truth. Blaming it on being young and immature would have been a disservice and wouldn't have helped me prevent the weeds from growing back again. In order to remove them once and for all, we had to get to their root and dig it up. The root revealed a longing to be affirmed by men, which exists because I wasn't affirmed by healthy, safe men throughout my upbringing.

Mirror holders are important on the journey of awareness. I have not found a more effective way to notice my shortcomings, bad habits, toxic cycles, or repressed emotions. Too often I look at a person or situation that is bothering me and judge them rather than looking inward to discover why these thoughts and feelings are emerging in me. Growing in my awareness lures me to no longer view other people as the problem and instead get curious about what it—any interaction or behavior that stirs up negative feelings—means for me. Now I know that, when confronted with a personality I find annoying or uncomfortable to be around, I have been given an opportunity to learn more about myself. This perspective shift helps me heal and understand the broken parts of myself.

In college, I seldom wore anything nicer than sweatpants or did something with my hair that required more effort than a messy bun. Much to my dismay, I had nearly every class with a gal who dressed adorably, wore her hair with gorgeously tousled curls, and always made time for mascara. One of my roommates started spending time with her, and the more she came around, the more I was annoyed. My roommate caught on to my disapproval and asked why I didn't like her friend. I shrugged my shoulders and said, "You know how some people just rub you the wrong way? She just does that to me." It was a pathetic cop-out of an answer. Now, many years later, I know exactly why she bothered me—and it had nothing to do with her, really. Her choice and ability to put herself together in a way I couldn't or chose not to made me jealous and insecure.

Awareness doesn't shrug its shoulders and make up excuses. Awareness faces the truth, no matter how annoying and embarrassing it may be.

This isn't just a thing of the past for me, either. Let me tell you— this work is ongoing. Not long ago I opened up to my mentor about how a friend was really hitting a nerve of mine with the things she was putting out for the world to see. At first, my mentor asked what was coming up for me whenever I saw and read this person's posts, and I didn't have an answer except that they really irked me. She asked me why, and I couldn't pinpoint it. Then my mentor wiped the mirror off so that it was squeaky-clean as she asked, "What is it about her that you see in *yourself?*"

I got offended. "Nothing! We're *nothing* alike," I firmly declared. She forced me to keep looking in the mirror. "Then why is it you're so bothered by her?"

After spending a long time looking in the mirror, I was able to explain what bothered me so much. I felt like she was making a mockery of foster care and misrepresenting foster parenting. Once I was able to look in the mirror and see clearly, I realized that a conversation with her was necessary if I wanted to keep following her without growing more resentful.

Viewing others—even friends and family who don't realize it— as mirror holders reflecting back to me what I often didn't see is productive, because I can work on myself in an area that, sooner or later, a situation will provoke out of me.

Whether you knew it before reading this chapter or not, you are a mirror for others. At all times, we are both the student and the teacher in this life. Think about your behaviors: What have you said and done just in the last week? Reflect on moments you felt irritated and identify what triggered that emotion. What lessons have you offered others? What have you possibly revealed for someone else? When we choose awareness, we must be prepared to face things that are awkward. Becoming more aware is no walk in the park. In my personal experience, it's much more of a well-paced marathon.

2. Therapy

In college I developed swollen lymph nodes under my armpits, insomnia, unexplained rapid weight loss, and other strange physical symptoms. The doctor ordered bloodwork, but everything came back perfectly normal. I felt frustrated that I was feeling sick and having these signs of illness, yet there was no clear, treatable diagnosis. Around the same time, I started talking to a counselor on campus because they offered several free sessions to students, and I rarely pass up a free opportunity! I didn't bring up my physical health because I wasn't there to talk about that. But wouldn't you know, we ended up working through some resentment I had been harboring—and within a month all of my physical symptoms were gone. My lymph nodes returned to normal, I went back to sleeping like a rock, and my weight stabilized. I hadn't been aware that my unresolved bitterness was eating away at me, literally. My body had reacted to all that my mind and soul were carrying. There is undoubtedly a direct connection between mind and body wellness. Conflict, trauma, and stress will reveal themselves outwardly if we don't deal with them internally.

I once saw a quote floating around online that read, "I'm in therapy to learn how to deal with people who should be in therapy," and it made me chuckle. Sometimes I attend therapy for myself, and other times I go solely because I don't know how to deal with someone else's issues and how they are affecting me.

Personally, some specific benefits of attending therapy have included

- Sharing my story in a safe space and having a neutral person validate my experience and point out connections I hadn't made before. For example, how a negative belief I have about myself is directly tied to something a trusted adult said to me when I was twelve years old.
- Receiving bite-sized action steps to move forward on a goal that feels overwhelming or entirely impossible. For

example, how to stop being easily provoked and losing my composure—it's been a journey, but I've made enormous progress and developed skills to channel my anger in healthy, appropriate ways.

- Creating more fulfilling relationships. All of my relationships are better when I am pursuing wholeness.

Therapy is a tool for self-awareness, but it's also so much more. It can improve all areas of life. If you feel like something is holding you back from living life to the fullest, therapy will address this. When you aren't sure what's keeping you from making change, therapy will help you discover the answer. Even if you aren't sure you want to commit to therapy, many therapists offer a free consultation to talk through what you're dealing with.[3]

3. The Enneagram

We can't be self-aware without knowing ourselves really well . . . not who we wish we were or some cleaned-up version of ourselves, but who we are in real time. If you have yet to take the Enneagram test to find out what type you are, I strongly suggest you do so (more on this in chapter 6). It is not a personality test; rather, it is an assessment that, if taken honestly, reveals your most prominent fears and desires. When used as intended, the Enneagram can help you understand why you are the way you are and see the goodness of God in yourself.

The most fun part about the Enneagram is discovering your gifts, your strengths, and which attributes of God are most obvious in you. The less fun but equally crucial part about it is recognizing your struggles, temptations, bad habits, and repeated cycles. The Enneagram is helpful with this because every type has a healthy/unhealthy scale, so if you are honest, you will inevitably begin to identify both the beauty and the ugliness inside your soul.

In a time where "self-love" is all the rage, I like to remind people that self-love without self-awareness is delusional and destructive.

We need both. One without the other is like a compass with a broken needle—we can't use it to get where we want to go. Think about it like this: if I am full of self-awareness but don't have self-love, I'll beat myself up constantly, lack confidence, and search for love in all of the wrong places. If I am full of self-love but don't have self-awareness, I'll probably be ignorant, prideful, stagnant, and have tons of blind spots. We are at our best when we have both self-love and self-awareness. The Enneagram is a beautiful tool for discovering both at the same time.

4. Journaling

One of the most underrated steps to developing deeper introspective awareness is keeping a good old-fashioned journal. Writing is a lot like meditating because it forces your mind to get clear about what you are thinking and feeling. As author Flannery O'Connor reportedly said, "I write because I don't know what I think until I read what I say."[4]

I used to think it was quite funny how often I'd receive a DM on Instagram or an email that started with, "I'm sure you're really busy and don't have time to read this or reply, but I wanted to share . . ." and by the end of it sometimes they'd thank me and say that just writing it all out seemed to help. They were sharing things with me and seeking my advice even though they knew I may never see their message or reply, simply because we all feel better when we process. Oddly enough, we often don't think to write or type out our situation, thoughts, or feelings unless there's someone on the other side waiting for it, and we can expect a response. However, it's not about anyone reading what we have to say or replying to it. We gain perspective simply in the process.

Journaling is super simple but highly effective. Whether you make confessions aloud to another human being or jot them down on the page before going to sleep, it's important to make space for your emotions and to release what you regret so it doesn't weigh you down.

If you ever reread old journal entries, you will find that sometimes your words will comfort you and other times they will convict you. Often my own words surprise me, and I think that's because the Spirit was actually writing them through me. I enjoy tracking personal growth not by the goals I achieved but by reading my old journals and noticing how much more aware and emotionally intelligent I've become.

Know Yourself Intimately

Hopefully by now you realize that there are a variety of tools available to those who wish to become more aware. Some are free, others are inexpensive, and there are some that require a greater investment.

Free tools
  Meditate
  Do a SWOT assessment (strengths, weaknesses, opportunities, and threats)
  Watch TED Talks
  Listen to podcasts that provoke reflection
  Keep a diary
  Practice mindfulness exercises
  Use a feelings wheel (google one to see what I mean)
  Seek feedback from trusted people in your life
Inexpensive tools
  Read books on self-awareness and emotional intelligence
  Take personality assessments such as Myers-Briggs and the Enneagram
Greater investments
  Attend therapy
  Participate in a guided retreat

After gaining knowledge of who we are and why we show up in the world the way we do, we are compelled to action. Without action, our growth is grossly limited, which is a shame because there is so much beauty ahead. In the pages to follow, I'll hold up a mirror and ask you to be honest about what you see, share outward exercises that lead toward inward discovery, and equip you with tangible steps to choose radical honesty that leads to real healing.

If we confess our sins, he is faithful and just and will forgive us our sins and purify us from all unrighteousness. (1 John 1:9)

SOUL CARE PRACTICE NO. 2
Develop a habit of confession.

Be Radically Honest with Yourself

1. Who can you go to when you need to get something off your chest?

2. What is a negative belief you have about yourself, and why do you believe it?

3. What has been said about you that makes you defensive, and why do you think that is?

4. What do you suspect people say about you when you're not around?

5. What stands in the way of you getting to know yourself better?

CHAPTER 3

What's *Really* Going On

During the COVID-19 pandemic of 2020, Eric and I started watching what we thought was a lighthearted comedy, *Atypical*, on Netflix. The show is centered around a teenager on the autism spectrum, Sam, and his family. It was all feel-good at first, but then the plotline got real in a way we weren't expecting (spoiler alert). In the show, Sam's mom, Elsa, has an affair with a man she meets at a bar. It isn't long before she's caught, and the affair is exposed to her husband, Doug, and their children. After some time, her husband agrees to go with her to couple's counseling so they can attempt to navigate forgiveness and healing and ultimately restore their marriage. In many ways, the show was triggering for me because, while our stories are different, the counseling sessions felt deeply familiar.

In one episode, Doug and Elsa are in their counselor's office, and he asks his wife how it happened. She admits that it all started with a little white lie. She recalls a specific instance when she had been daydreaming about a man (the one she ended up having an affair with), but when asked by her husband what was on her mind, she made something up. She didn't say, "Oh, I was just daydreaming about this hot guy I met," probably because she was embarrassed and most likely told herself it was "just" a crush. More than anything, I'm assuming, she didn't want to hurt her husband by admitting she had someone else on her mind. However, as the show reveals and my own personal experience proves, when we aren't radically honest we only hurt ourselves and everyone we love most. Yes, it's awkward to admit when you fantasize about someone who isn't your spouse, but surely it's much more awkward to later confess you have acted on that fantasy. Radical honesty is an important piece of the journey toward real healing. One lie almost always leads to another . . . and a web of lies leaves you tangled and frantic for an escape.

Counseling was the start of my healing journey and has been an enormous, ongoing part of my life ever since. Through counseling I was able to retrace my steps and notice where things went wrong. It was clear that my fall began years prior to the incident I kept secret due to shame. With the help of my counselor, I retraced my steps all the way back to childhood.

I grew up in a divorced home, spending every other weekend at my dad's. Most of the time he wasn't there because he was married to his job, and so I spent those weekends with my abusive stepmother, Sharon. Eventually she and my dad had a kid together: my half-sister, Haylee, who is seven and a half years younger than me. Throughout my childhood, I went to my dad's house every other weekend only to spend those seventy-two hours with a stepmom who despised me and took all of her anger and rage out on me. A closet alcoholic, she is the reason my mathematics skills were excellent early on. You see, I would keep a close watch on the clock, counting down the hours, minutes, and sometimes seconds until my mom came to pick me up.

I didn't tell anyone what was happening at my dad's house, not even my mom, who I truly believe is the greatest mother in the world. I didn't want to cause trouble or create turmoil between them. Like many kids from divorced homes, I played the role of peacekeeper so that coparenting wouldn't be so dramatic and difficult for my parents. I also didn't say anything about what was happening behind my dad's back because I subconsciously believed that he might not believe me or, even worse, would pick Sharon over me. I couldn't bear the thought of losing him completely.

Children are smarter and more emotionally aware than we often give them credit for. Inside of me was a huge void, a longing for my daddy. For him to simply be around, even if he was tired from work and just needed a nap. For him to play with me, show up to my gymnastics meets, and hear from my teachers how well I was doing in school. Everything I did, I did to make him proud in hopes that it would make him love me. I often heard him tell me he loved me, actually, but I rarely felt that love. *How can you love someone if you don't ever want to spend time with them?* Because of our strained relationship and the hole in my heart desperately wanting to be filled, I turned to other men, seeking their love and acceptance. Most of the time they gave me desire and attention disguised as love and acceptance. This meant I grew up confusing desire for love. Love is a biological need, whereas desire is a motivation.

Desire says I want *you*.

Love says I want *what's best for* you.

Notice the subtle yet powerful difference?

In high school and throughout college, I got really good at seeking the attention of men to fill the void. I did it so subtly that no one knew. Or if they noticed at all, they probably didn't say much, because it's awkward to approach someone with destructive behaviors when they have no awareness that they are being self-destructive at all. I was a closet addict, just like Sharon, only alcohol wasn't my vice. I didn't actually *want* to have sex with anyone, but I teased guys and led them to believe I would do anything they wanted, because that's what kept them hanging out with me longer and texting me more often. I wanted to be wanted so badly that I went to great lengths to feel desired.

Soul Care to Save Your Life

Counseling did not justify or excuse my past behaviors—it gave me an honest look at everything that led me into the dark. They say history repeats itself, which is true unless we acknowledge it honestly. This is why it's important to pay attention and dig beneath the surface so that we don't repeat our worst moments.

To this day, Eric and I proactively attend counseling together in an effort to stay on top of our relational health. This is no different than going to the doctor for a checkup to care for our physical health. We love our counselor because she is so helpful and encouraging. She equips us with tools to navigate difficult situations and come out of them more united. Similar to having me retrace my personal journey, she has Eric and me dig deep and get to the root of every issue we bring into her office.

It's Not about the Mayo

One of our biggest blowups as a married couple was over a sandwich. I wish I were kidding. It was a Saturday afternoon, and we wanted to grab tacos from our favorite spot but were on a strict "no eating out" budget, so we stayed home. While making himself a turkey and cheese sandwich, he hollered, "Do you want a sandwich, babe?" to which I thought, *Have I ever turned down food?* I hollered back, "Yes, please. Thanks!"

He plopped down on the gray chair next to me, handing me the sandwich. One bite in, I asked, "Honey, this is so dry. What all is on it?"

Rolling his eyes, he answered, "Turkey, cheese, lettuce, and tomato."

"What's on yours?" I asked defensively.

"Same as yours . . . a little more meat . . . plus mayo . . ." His voice trailed off.

At that, a switch flipped inside me. "Why didn't you put mayo on mine?" I asked, raising my voice.

"Because you don't usually like mayo on your sandwiches."

50

"What do you mean I don't like mayo? Since when? Do you even know me?"

As quickly as the weather in Chicago changes, so did the results of this thoughtful gesture from my husband. Because he felt attacked and I was defensive, something minuscule escalated to tears and silence—a whole day of not speaking to each other over a *sandwich*, for crying out loud! *What is wrong with us?* I wondered.

When we decided to talk again, it was because Eric really wanted to watch our show together (*Breaking Bad . . .* so binge-worthy), so he apologized for upsetting me and not putting mayo on my sandwich. I laughed and apologized for getting so mad over something so dumb as mayonnaise. We moved on and put the incident behind us.

That is, until we walked into our appointment with our favorite lady, our counselor, just a few days later. Like every session, she began with a smile and the general question, "So, how are you two?"

We told her we were doing well and mentioned our ridiculous sandwich tiff. She pressed in, asking questions about what happened. We answered and assured her we were past it. We expressed that we would rather spend our time discussing more important things, like upcoming major decisions regarding the children in our care. But, being the wonderful counselor she is, she didn't let up. She looked at us sternly, and firmly stated, "It's not about the mayo!" which left us looking at each other, puzzled. We were like a pair of toddlers being schooled. And in terms of marriage, we were toddlers, with just a couple years of marriage under our belt at the time. She helped us identify that our fight wasn't about the thing we were arguing over. It was deeper, an issue that couldn't be seen but lived beneath the surface. The root of this conflict was my fear that my own husband didn't know me, along with the even deeper root of feeling unseen and abandoned by all males in my life. Her questions and guidance in leading us to this realization are evidence that counselors are some of the best mirror holders.

Have you experienced a stupid disagreement or silly argument with your significant other, parent, or a friend that led to a massive blowup? While it might feel better in the moment to just say sorry and "get through it," there are consequences of bypassing radical honesty and healthy conflict. When we neglect to find the root, we miss an opportunity to better ourselves and our relationships. I'd go as far as to say that when we make peace without acknowledging our truth, we prolong the inevitable: an explosion built on increasing tension. Instead of suppressing, we need to uproot the rotting, dead root in all areas of our lives. Before we can uproot it, we have to be aware that there is one and find a good mirror holder to guide us in discovering what it is and how we can dig it up. After all, it's rarely about the mayo.

Band-Aid Approach

As a child, I was constantly in motion. Cartwheeling, flipping, climbing, running . . . there was no shortage of energy from my scrawny younger self. When I was around five years old, I loved to play on this old rickety playset in our backyard, and I would spend hours teaching myself tricks on its bars. One time, while straddling the high bar and gripping it firmly with both hands, I leaned forward to twirl around and around like I always did. Only this time, I must have gotten dizzy or my palms must have gotten sweaty, because I slipped and tumbled down. My face took quite a blow, and there was a huge gash on one side of my mouth. My mom was mowing the lawn, and when she came around the corner, she found me lying in the grass and crying hysterically as blood pooled around my mouth. She rushed to my aid in a panic and whisked me off to the hospital, where I was treated with a dose of pain medication and five gnarly stitches. The doctor assured my mom that her Gym Monkey Manda (a nickname I loved at the time) would heal in no time. He didn't exaggerate; I was fully healed in just a couple of weeks. To this day, if I point it out, you can see the faint scar where the trauma occurred, but otherwise there weren't any long-term implications. Doctors and modern medicine are such a gift.

Imagine though, if my mom had tried to put a Band-Aid over the deep cut on the corner of my mouth. Instead of stitches, a Band-Aid. On a wound that's split wide open, gushing blood, it wouldn't have been effective. Even if the bleeding stopped, the gash wouldn't have closed or completely healed. Most likely it would have continued splitting back open, maybe healing improperly and resulting in future struggles when speaking or eating.

It's easy for us to comprehend how a deep physical wound cannot be treated with a Band-Aid, but for some reason we have a harder time understanding this when it comes to emotional and relational wounds. Instead of getting stitches for a deep cut, treating a burn with cream, or removing the bullet from our spleen, we slap a Band-Aid on, convincing ourselves that we will heal up just the same—not considering the repercussions of this approach.

I've seen it time and time again in both my own life and the lives of people I love most. We don't address the thing our friend nonchalantly said that really bothered us, because we'd rather avoid conflict. We don't question why we keep running into the arms of people who are no good for us and instead find every reason to justify our behavior. We pretend things are fine when they are not, because it feels awkward and wonky to admit the truth. We suppress instead of uprooting, because it's safe and comfortable. **Until it's not.** That's the sneaky thing about the Band-Aid approach. It works *until* the wound gets an infection or is poked at. I saw this firsthand with one of my closest friends.

Sarah and I had the kind of friendship where we didn't feel the need to clean the toilet when the other was on her way over, even if there were skid marks in it. We always welcomed each other to drop by on the fly. We loved meeting up at each other's houses, going to cafés, and trying new restaurants. We enjoyed weekly dinners together and laughed about ridiculous things our husbands would say. I cheered her on as she launched her own business, and she popped a bottle of champagne when I got my first book deal. She had a panic attack on my kitchen floor, and I wept on her living room couch. She was by my side when we took in our first foster child and accompanied me to multiple doctor appointments. Though we were opposite in many ways, we went together like cookies and milk. Sisters by choice, always better together.

I'm not sure when things began changing between us, because they didn't change for me. But one day this friend I loved so deeply abruptly cut me out of her life. Just before what would end up being our final conversation, I was made aware that she had unfollowed me on social media. When I went to see for myself, it was true. I was so confused. At this point, I wasn't aware of any quarrel between us. She had even dropped off a little something to me a few days prior. So, to my knowledge, Sarah was still my ride-or-die bestie.

Maybe it was an accidental unfollow, I pondered over the social media discovery.

I talked with Eric about it, who assured me that social media is not real life and not to give it another thought. While I appreciated his ability to bring things to a mature place, I also reminded him that in this day and age, it was weird to unfollow your own best friend. I thought it had to be an accident, so I shot her a text.

> Hey . . . awkward, I noticed you unfollowed me on social media. Totally an accident, right? Or is there something we need to talk about?

She replied, which led to a few more text messages, and then we finally grew up and got on the phone like adults.

Conflict doesn't bother me; in fact, I am often energized by it. However, the conversation Sarah and I had was vague and confusing. There wasn't one specific thing she referred to that helped me make sense of her explanation as to why she deliberately unfollowed me on social media. She simply shared that I made her "uncomfortable." She thought she could preserve our friendship by no longer following me on social media. Her words "preserve our friendship" still bring tears to my eyes. This was a new boundary for her, she explained.

When we hung up, I was dumbfounded. *Did I make her uncomfortable in person too, or only online? How was our friendship rocky and I didn't even notice? Why didn't she come to me and talk about this?* I felt blindsided. While I am all for boundaries, this felt more like a dagger than a line in the sand. A passive-aggressive move to get me to discover that something was wrong. I took a deep inhale and slowly let it out.

Imagine your closest friend dropping a bomb like that out of nowhere. Apparently I made her uncomfortable, but I didn't have any examples of something I said or did to help me understand when this was happening. She unfollowed me without discussing any of this with me until I approached her myself. Was this betrayal, or was I still missing something? All I knew is that the solid ground I had been standing on was now shattered into pieces.

I may never know for sure what was shifting inside of Sarah beneath the surface of our friendship in the days, weeks, maybe even months that led to our falling out, but what I believe with every fiber in my being is that we could've worked through it. Sweeping dirt under the rug is useless because it's still there, only hidden. Instead of hiding dirt, we can use the same amount of energy to sweep it up into a dustpan, dump it in the trash, and then take that garbage out. By uprooting what was wrong instead of suppressing it, Sarah and I probably wouldn't have experienced a fallout. Our friendship didn't have to end like it did . . . and maybe it didn't have to end at all.

Identify the Root

When a tree is producing bad fruit, it can be traced back to its roots. Are they getting enough water? Is there enough sunlight? How's the soil? What other organisms are nearby?

The same is true for each of us. If we notice gossip, envy, gluttony, and other bad fruit showing up in our lives, we need to ask ourselves some questions. *Am I spending time with God? How am I taking care of myself? Have I been honest? Do I express gratitude? How could I be more intentional and proactive? Who am I surrounding myself with?* These questions guide us to consider the things that are in our control and to look at our roots with a magnifying glass.

If we desire to be more whole, conscious humans who live radically honest lives in the light, we have to stop ignoring, justifying, or pretending we don't have struggles. Whether it be envy, anger, fabricating, or something entirely different, we can choose to eradicate these bad fruits from our lives if we are willing to get to their roots. We need to ask what is going on deep inside of our souls that leads us to make the bad decisions or continue the bad habits.

It might seem to help temporarily to hit the unfollow button, isolate yourself from anyone who is more (or less) successful than you are, or write off your behavior as "just the way" you are, but none of those are real solutions. They are merely Band-Aids on infections that long to be healed.

And I promise you: healing is possible if you get to the root.

The Difference between Change and Transformation

Every eight weeks or so, I sit in my favorite chair with a black cloak around my neck as my hairstylist, Erin, works her magic on my hair. I've had it colored dark brown, a shade of red, caramel highlights, and most frequently, bright blonde. I choose whichever color I want, and Erin will change my hair to it if I'm willing to sit still for a few hours and fork over half a paycheck. I leave with a new look every single time, but it doesn't last. Erin isn't able to replace the hair God gave me; she can't transform the hair growing out of my scalp. Within a couple of months, the natural roots of my hair always grow out, displaying my light brown color.

Similarly, no matter how much I appreciate a fun British accent, I'm never going to have one. Even if I deliberately speak with one for the rest of my days—an effort that would probably become annoying very quickly—it would merely be a performance. Certain things, like where we grow up and the way we sound when we speak, are not in our control and cannot be transformed.

Change is temporary; transformation is ongoing. Change is something we strive for; transformation is what happens when we stop striving. Change happens on the surface; transformation requires getting to the root.

Behavior modification and Band-Aid approaches are fine if you want a life that feels inauthentic and is constantly full of relational turnover. But if you want something different—if you want a life that's healed and full of forgiveness—then the invitation to transform is for you.

[Jesus] went on: "What comes out of a person is what defiles them. For it is from within, out of a person's heart, that evil thoughts come—sexual immorality, theft, murder, adultery, greed, malice, deceit, lewdness, envy, slander, arrogance and folly. All these evils come from inside and defile a person." (Mark 7:20–23)

SOUL CARE PRACTICE NO. 3
Dig a layer deeper to find the root.

Be Radically Honest with Yourself

1. What are you afraid may be true about yourself?
2. What unhealthy patterns exist in your life?
3. Who have you decided to cancel, and why?
4. Where are you striving and falling short?
5. When have you slapped on a Band-Aid when you actually needed stitches?

CHAPTER 4

The One Thing That Changes Everything

I've spent most of my life getting it all wrong, striving to impress, and fumbling my way around the truth. Since we're all about honesty here, one of my only qualifications for writing this book is that I am willing to put it all on the line. If radical honesty and the practices of soul care weren't worth telling the world about, I'd keep my dirty laundry in the hamper and carry on. Some days I'd rather do that, but it's worth exposing the mess and baring the worst of myself to reveal all God has done to save me and enrich my life.

False Allegations

It was our fourth "yes" in foster care. A lot has happened since— including a dozen more yeses—but I remember this one like it happened just yesterday.

Around midnight a text popped up on my phone asking if we were available to take in an emergency placement of two children directly from Lurie Children's Hospital in Chicago, where we were living at the time. Only a couple of hours prior I had expressed to Eric that I was so thankful for a break from kids and was excited to sleep in the next morning. As if the universe heard us and laughed, that text pinged my cell, and my tune changed entirely. Eric lovingly questioned me, "Are you sure you want to take in these two kids, babe?" to which I replied, "I'm sure these kids don't want to be in this situation, but they didn't get a choice. At least we have one. It's a yes for me. You in?" He smiled and said, "Always." Within a few minutes we were on the phone with a caseworker, learning more about the request, and then we were lacing up our shoes to head over to the hospital for the pickup.

Upon arriving at the hospital, we were escorted to a room where two children, one boy and one girl, were sleeping in a bed together. There was a strong, foul smell of urine, but no one mentioned it. I walked over to the bed and, as always happens, fell in love at first sight. I have yet to meet a child in need of a temporary loving home who doesn't have my whole heart immediately. We had to gently wake them up, awkwardly introduce ourselves as their foster parents, and load them into our vehicle to bring them back to our home, where they would be staying for God only knew how long—literally. The hospital social worker and case manager did their best to help them understand that we were a "nice couple" who would be taking care of them "for a while," but it was clear the children were exhausted and scared. After signing some legal documents and receiving hospital goody bags for the kids that contained a teddy bear, toothbrush, and T-shirt, we were off.

The drive home was silent and awkward. Because it was nearly 2:00 a.m., Eric and I didn't want to exhaust the kids with a million questions like, "What's your favorite food?" or "Do you want to take a bath before you go to bed?" so we said very little. I read through the paperwork, trying to absorb all of the information that would be helpful, such as their full names, ages, and any food allergies.

When we got home, they went straight to bed and so did we, but I couldn't sleep. There was a heaviness weighing on my heart. I was sad for these kids. I knew they needed to come into care based on what little information I was given, but I was sad that they were with us—complete strangers with a spare bedroom for kids like them.

Although I didn't get to sleep in like I'd been looking forward to for so long, the next morning was a huge relief. I was worried the kids might wake up scared and confused since they hadn't been totally awake or coherent throughout the transition into our care from the hospital, but it was the complete opposite. We were greeted with hugs, and no one put up a fight when I suggested bathing. They were adjusting extremely well in their new environment.

Very soon after they came into our care, we received information about their mom and were given the green light to make contact and set up a visit. This was great news. We arranged for the mom to meet us at a Skyzone so she could engage with her kids in a fun environment instead of awkwardly sitting across from them at a fast-food joint.

On the day of the visit, our caseworker texted that she wasn't going to be able to make it to the visit but felt comfortable with us supervising it without her, and we wouldn't have to reschedule. We'd supervised visitation many times before, so this wasn't a big deal. We went, and the visit happened as planned. Skyzone was a huge hit. Their mom showed up, jumped on the trampoline with her kids, and engaged with me and Eric. Like many of the parents I first meet after reading all that they've done "wrong" on paper, I was pleasantly surprised at how kind and natural our interactions were. I had a sense that she was going to be one of our most organic partnerships in the world of foster care to date.

When it was time to leave, the kids hugged her goodbye, and I prepared internally for their meltdown, which typically happens regardless of whether a visit goes well or not. To my surprise, their mom asked if she could drive them back to our home just to have a little bit of extra time with them. The kids began pleading with us, and nothing in my gut felt "off." I mean, after all, this was their mother. So we agreed to let her drive them back to our apartment building, even though it was technically not approved by our caseworker.

When they pulled up to our building a few minutes after us, a rush of relief came over me. You see, as Eric and I were driving home, discussing how great the visit went and how well the kids were doing, I began to worry about a bunch of what-if situations. *What if the mom takes off with the kids? What if we get in big trouble for letting her drive them without one of us being in the car? What if someone gets hurt?*

Yet as soon as their mom got out of her vehicle, it was apparent something had shifted. Her demeanor was no longer approachable or calm. She walked straight over to me on the sidewalk, got right up in my face, and began shouting about how I'd slapped her daughter across the face. I was wildly confused and taken aback. Eric and I tried to deescalate the situation so that we could understand where her accusations were coming from. At the same time, we were trying to get the kids inside so they wouldn't witness this very heated interaction. Our attempts were useless. Everything blew up. Nothing was making any sense, but it was obvious peace wasn't possible. She kept repeating that when we weren't around on the car ride home, her kids had told her about me slapping one of them, and that she was going to make sure I paid for it. It ended with a phone call to our caseworker, the mom storming off, and us following instructions to take the children and their belongings to a different foster home. I was an emotional wreck. The kids seemed numb.

After dropping them off to their new placement, we got on the phone with our caseworker, who assured us that everything would be OK . . . eventually. She told us that for the time being we were simply to carry on with our lives until an investigation could clear us of the allegation their mother had threatened to report. Apparently, the story was that I was a child abuser and had slapped her four-year-old daughter across the face. How on God's green earth was I supposed to "carry on as normal" while I waited to hear about this possible investigation? If the investigation happened, how could it prove that I was a fit, safe, and appropriate foster parent? Would it simply be her word against mine? Could we lose our license over this? What did the kids think was really going on? I hated that they only got such a small amount of rest with us before getting traumatized all over again. I wasn't sure about any of it. And it was hell.

Weeks went by, and we heard nothing. I sent emails inquiring about the whole ordeal and finally received word that everything had "blown over," and I was cleared of the allegations. *That's it?* I thought. This felt so unfair and cruel. I was offered a brief explanation that this particular mother was known for making big claims about the foster parents who cared for her kids. (That was supposed to make me feel better?) I didn't receive the type of closure a person should get when they are falsely accused of abusing a child, but I was relieved to be done with the situation.

Despite how terrifying it was, Eric and I didn't throw in the towel on foster care after that. We learned a huge lesson, however: don't bend the rules, because it may create an opportunity for a lie to be drummed up . . . or worse.

Can you imagine if I had been deemed guilty, we lost our license to foster, or, even worse, I had to serve time in jail for child abuse, all because of a false allegation? Even worse than being falsely accused is being wrongly convicted. Sadly, that's exactly what happened to Ronald Cotton in 1984.

Jennifer Thompson was raped at knifepoint by a man who broke into her apartment while she slept. Three days after the brutal rape, Jennifer was led through a flawed photographic lineup that caused a mistaken eyewitness ID that put Ronald behind bars. After serving eleven years in prison for a crime he never committed, Ronald was released when a DNA test proved his innocence.[1]

Two years after being released from prison for a crime he did not commit, Ronald met the woman who wrongly accused him, Jennifer, face-to-face. She felt unbelievably guilty and ashamed. Her mistake cost him his dignity, his reputation, and eleven years of his life that couldn't be given back.

Ronald could've demanded reparations. He could've cussed her out or done a number of things to this woman who'd robbed him of so much. Instead, he chose a radical path. He accepted her apology and forgave her. He demonstrated the undeserved, life-altering grace of Jesus. Because of grace, both of them were able to access healing and freedom. If that isn't crazy enough, the two of them went on to become friends and wrote a bestselling memoir telling their unique story!

Forgiveness does not always lead to friendship, but it does shatter shame. Forgiveness replaces shame with honor—not only for the person on the receiving end but for the person offering it as well. I'm sure Jennifer felt enormous guilt and shame when she learned of her horrific mistake in identifying the wrong person as her rapist. We can only imagine the emotions she felt in the two years between Ronald's release and their in-person meeting. The most beautiful thing is how Ronald refused to let shame rob Jennifer of her life in the same way she had mistakenly robbed him. Where there was justified anger, guilt, and shame, God brought forgiveness, peace, and friendship, despite none of it making sense. That is a picture of grace—radical, shame-shattering, life-altering grace.

Experiencing Grace for Yourself

Much like the abundant forgiveness I received from my husband and the unparalleled, extraordinary forgiveness Ronald gave to Jennifer, we all will experience what it is like to be both the giver and the recipient of grace at various points in our lives.

The tangible relief of grace can't adequately be put into words but is best experienced for yourself. Sure, you get a taste of grace when you've been snippy with someone you love yet they forgive you—no harm, no foul. You also get a taste of grace if you cancel last-minute plans with a friend who has every right to be frustrated but instead chooses to let you off the hook. In both of those situations, the offense is not going to cause the end of the relationship unless it recurs often. When the stakes are higher, however, and you do something that jeopardizes the relationship, it results in a desperate ache for grace that is vastly more consequential. It's the difference between grace that's wanted so things can be right again and grace that's needed so you can simply live with yourself. I know, because I've been the one clamoring for much more than a taste of grace.

When I told the full truth to my husband about my struggles with wanting attention from other men and how it had spiraled, I was buried in shame. I fully anticipated him to be angry and cold with me. I was terrified he would leave, and life as we knew it would be over. Instead, what he said and how he acted toward me made our healing possible.

I still couldn't believe the first words out of his mouth were, "I still love you." In that very moment and in the days that followed, Eric was slow to speak and cautious with each question he asked. In the midst of feeling his own pain, which I'd caused, he never threatened to leave me, and he remained gentle in our interactions. After learning that I had made an irrevocable mistake and navigating his own valid feelings of betrayal, Eric offered a gracious response and went on a journey of forgiving me that saved our marriage. Later on came the rebuilding of trust and intimacy that allowed our marriage to thrive again, but that's for another book.

My life, his life, and this book would be entirely different if my husband had chosen revenge or decided to call it quits. He could have done either and probably felt better—at least for the moment—but instead he embraced me and told me there wasn't anything I could ever tell him that would make him walk away. I wasn't sure I believed him all the times before when he'd said those clichéd promises, but now I knew he really meant them.

Grace saved our marriage and most definitely saved my life.

New Life

We cared for our big boys, Bear and Skittles, for nearly two years. Then, just forty-eight hours after we transitioned them into their pre-adoptive home, our biological son, Shia Grace Carpenter, was born. On February 17, 2021, weighing just 5 lbs. 3 oz., our tiny peanut made an early debut. I called him Birdie for the first month, since he made adorable chirp-like noises and constantly moved his lips toward me, signaling, "Feed me, Mama."

Shia was deeply wanted and chosen. I vividly remember the weekend we went for a walk and decided we were ready to stop preventing pregnancy. It seemed like the entire city awoke from its slumber, which is what happens on the first beautiful spring day after a bitter cold winter in Chicago. We strolled through the park chatting about our upcoming anniversary, reflecting on how far we'd come. We had changed cities, jobs, and a lot of our political views. We then went through a long season of confession, counseling, and repairing our relationship. Later, we chose to play a part in raising a ton of other people's children through foster care, buy our first home, and create meaningful resources to help other young married couples. Our life together was stable, and our marriage had a strong foundation. Not the counterfeit "strong" foundation some have simply because nothing bad or crazy has happened, but the bona fide strong foundation we'd built by choice.

Eric always knew he wanted a biological child, but I wasn't so sure. For a long time, I said "never" or "no way" whenever the topic came up. But our fostering journey led me to have a change of heart, and I became open to it. I loved motherhood and knew for sure that I wanted to have permanent children in our care, but I wanted to continue fighting for family preservation and reunification. This conundrum led to many discussions with my therapist and mentor and, ultimately, the realization that I didn't have to choose. It was another situation where either/or needed to be considered from a both/and lens. We stopped preventing pregnancy *and* continued raising the two boys who were temporarily placed in our care.

I learned I was pregnant in the bathroom of a Meijer supermarket because I couldn't wait a second to take the test on the first day of my missed period. Shock, anxiety, and joy filled my soul when I saw the two lines appear. I can usually hardly produce tears, but in that moment the floodgates opened. It wasn't long before we began to discuss names. As our first biological child and possibly the only child we would ever get to name, choosing a name for our son was an arduous process.

We landed on Shia because we prefer unique, less common names and appreciated its Hebrew origin meaning "praise God." We chose the middle name Grace because it represents everything we want for him and serves as a testament to all that God has done and continues to do in our marriage.

Grace has a way of bringing about new life.

I Love You More Than That Dish

Some people think I'm nuts to meet up with folks I only know from the internet, but some of my greatest friendships have happened thanks to Instagram.

A few years ago, I booked a flight from Chicago to San Diego to spend time with my Instagram bestie, Anjuli. A fellow writer, wife, and mom, Anjuli was bound to be an easy hang, and I couldn't wait to chat with her face-to-face after years of comments, DMs, and voxing back and forth.

From the minute she picked me up at the airport, we hit it off. It was as if I'd just found my long-lost sister. She drove us to a beautiful spot to hike that overlooked the ocean. Our conversation was all over the place because there was so much ground to cover! Most of what we learn is caught not taught—and I learn a lot by surrounding myself with women like Anjuli. She is a mother to five beautiful humans and is incredibly intentional with them. Composure, gentleness, and patience ooze out of her, especially when she's parenting. I'm not so naïve as to think that Anjuli never loses her cool or feels overwhelmed like the rest of us, so this isn't to say I hold her on a pedestal (where none of us belong), it's just that when I'm with her I pay attention. The way of Jesus is her mission, and it's evident that produces a life overflowing with goodness.

During our hike, Anjuli and I both laughed and cried as we shared vulnerably the high highs and low lows of our unique motherhood journeys. She began reminiscing about how gracious her mom was when she was growing up and how she aspired to be the same kind of mom. She told me that when she was a little girl, the thing she remembers most is that if she or one of her siblings made a mess or broke something, like a dish, the first words out of her mom's mouth were always, "I love you more than that dish!" With tears in her eyes, Anjuli shared how comforting it was to grow up with a mom who loved her more than any material possession in their home and especially more than any mistake she made. Her mom's unconditional love cultivated a deep confidence within her and eliminated shame in her darkest moments.

Within a few weeks of my trip to San Diego and hearing Anjuli's story, my oldest son at the time, Goof, lost his brand-new pair of prescription glasses. I had jumped through a million hoops in the child welfare system to get him those glasses, and he only had them in hand for less than twenty-four hours before losing them. So, naturally, I was irritated. My initial reaction wasn't awful, but it certainly wasn't, "I love you more than those glasses." However, my gut knew I should've responded differently, so I followed the nudge to reassure him a few hours later.

"I want you to know I love you more than those glasses. You know that, don't you?" I asked.

Silence. He shrugged his shoulders in a way that communicated, *I guess, but I don't believe you.*

My heart sank. I tried to eliminate the shame he felt over losing his new glasses and disappointing me, which was evident by the way he was responding.

"I shouldn't have reacted so strongly. They are just a pair of glasses, and I know you didn't mean to lose them," I explained.

"Yeah, I always screw up," he said with his head down.

"Honey, you do not always screw up," I assured him. "Making mistakes is inevitable, but in this case it was an accident. It's not like you did it on purpose! If anything, I should have told you how proud I am that you came right to me and told me you lost them. That had to have been difficult. I'm really sorry for how I reacted. You're a good kid, and losing a pair of glasses does not make you any less of a good kid. You didn't deserve my frustration. Will you forgive me?"

He looked up at me, unsure what to say. He then buried himself in my arms, and as I held him, I noticed how my scrawny boy was developing into a broad man. Relief washed over us both as his shame shattered and my mom-guilt disappeared.

Grace is necessary for all of us, and parenting amplifies that need more than anything else I've ever experienced. Nothing else has forced me to face my own pride and selfishness so frequently.

Some days I have to ask for forgiveness, which is humbling. Other days I have to extend forgiveness, including times it isn't asked for but is necessary for me to move forward, which tends to be even more humbling. Without these powerful, raw, and sometimes awkward interactions of apology and forgiveness, tensions rise, and we're held back from experiencing all that God desires for our relationships to thrive.

My boys need me to say, "I love you more than _____," as they are bound to make mistakes, damage property, and make choices I wish they hadn't. As parents, we have innumerable opportunities to do this. When my little one wants to "help" cook dinner, I can decide to love him more than convenience, the perfect recipe, or a clean countertop. When my middle child wants to play a game with me just as I've cozied up on the couch to finish a thrilling novel, I can decide to love him more than my own desire. When one of my oldest chose to quit college, I had to decide to love her more than I disagreed with her decision. It is not an easy thing, loving our kids sacrificially and gracefully. It's even harder to do it with random people we encounter throughout our days. Yet that is precisely how Jesus lived his life and instructs us to live ours.

I've seen firsthand how a home founded on grace can provide supernatural healing. I've seen it in myself, in my husband, and in a child who looks at us with tear-filled eyes, desperate to believe he is still loved after destroying part of our home in a fit of rage.

Grace is loving others when they dare us not to anymore.

We All Live Densely Layered Lives

There's not a single person you wouldn't love if you knew their story. It's a theory I've been putting to the test for years. I believe it's true, because no one is the sum of their worst mistakes.

Often, when I first meet someone, I'm amazed at how quickly my assumptions are proved to be inaccurate. Stories matter, and they provide context. It's why many of us are quick to defend people we love if someone's perception of them seems to be way off base or simply limited.

There's a card in the fun, wildly inappropriate game called "What's Your Meme?" that reads, "When your ex wants to get back together after you've already talked trash about them to your mom." It's funny because it's relatable. At some point we have all been upset with someone and expressed it to a parent or close friend whose loyalty to us blinds them to the full picture—like the possibility that we aren't entirely innocent or that whoever has upset us is more than the mistake they made. This is why I'm cautious when it comes to sharing relational hardships in my life with people who are biased toward me.

Take my sweet grandma, for example, who has such a deep and loyal love for me. If I tell her about a small hiccup in my marriage or about a really hard conversation I had with a friend, she forgets all of the really wonderful things about these people and gets really fired up on my behalf. Granny isn't hearing both sides of the story or considering that there's more context outside of the situation I'm venting about. The good thing is that I know she'll always take my side and validate my feelings, but what's not helpful is that she won't see things objectively or necessarily advocate for resolution.

One time I shared with Granny how a friend really hurt my feelings, and a few weeks later she texted me to ask why I'd just posted a picture with that friend on Instagram. (Yes, my Granny texts and is super active on the socials.) I responded, assuring her that my friend had apologized and we had worked through our conflict. But Granny didn't like it because she is protective of me. She couldn't fathom why I would give the relationship another chance after the hurt I'd experienced. She was assessing this person and my relationship based on limited knowledge. I was certain that if she were able to meet this friend and spend even an hour with her, she'd absolutely love her. Why? Because she would learn more of the story. She would experience a person beyond a moment they aren't proud of.

Grace isn't a popular choice. A lot of people, even family and friends you love deeply, won't always approve or applaud you for choosing grace. Do it anyway.

It's easy to write people off—to come to our own judgments and opinions—without seeking to know the whole story. I've caught myself doing this when I make assumptions and cast judgment on my unhoused neighbors, for example. I take a small nugget about a person and draw my own conclusions without ever really getting to know them. And it's a shame, because there's always more than meets the eye.

Cancel culture seems to be a growing trend, and it scares me because it's a graceless approach to life. Cancel culture does not choose curiosity and grace. Instead, it treats people as if they are disposable. Without ever talking about an issue, we disregard anyone who disappoints us or doesn't align with us on a political or spiritual level and, without so much as a goodbye, we cut them from our lives.

We no longer make an effort to work things out. Instead, we stop returning texts and phone calls. We unfollow them and avoid the Starbucks if we know we might bump into them there on Sunday mornings after church. We choose this because it feels less awkward and requires less time and energy than if we were to tell the truth about how we feel and why. It's an immature approach that solves nothing but is often what we settle for when we don't believe healthy conflict and grace are worth pursuing.

Rather than push people away or cut them off, we ought to first let them know how we're feeling and bring it into the light. A repaired relationship won't always be possible, but forgiveness is, and parting ways cordially is worth our efforts. Not only could it help that person change for the better but it just might spare the relationship from being severed. If you don't have any longtime friends, consider if you have engaged in this disconnection pattern as an unhealthy way of coping with conflict.

Relationships involve people with different life experiences, beliefs, and perspectives. To think that relationships should be all fun and ease with no real effort is unrealistic. We all live densely layered lives. An honest conversation goes a long way, and cutting all ties is rarely necessary. After all, no one is the sum of their worst moments, and withholding forgiveness only hurts us.

I could've held a grudge against my father for many years over what he did on my seventh birthday (more on that in chapter 8), and while it might have felt good for a little while—hurting him for hurting me—it would've been counterproductive. I've heard a lot of analogies about grudges, but one that has always resonated most for me says, "Holding on to a grudge is like holding on to an anchor and jumping into the sea. If you don't let go, you'll drown."

Don't let a mistake made steal your life. Don't let the way someone hurt you rob you of a bright future. Deliberately choose grace.

When I was at my lowest breaking point due to the struggles and sin I had become so entangled with, I couldn't imagine a life that felt free or was worth sticking around for. Yet here I am, writing, speaking, and attempting to point others to Jesus. There are so many differences between who I once was and who I am today, but the most palpable by far can be summed up in that one word. *Grace*. It changes everything. It's more powerful than revenge, grudges, and striving to be "good." It's arguably the greatest gift we could ever give or receive. It's life-altering and it rewrote my story, the most beautiful plot twist of all.

Grace is the secret sauce to a soul set free.

Who is a God like you,
    who pardons sin and forgives the transgression
    of the remnant of his inheritance?
You do not stay angry forever
    but delight to show mercy.
You will again have compassion on us;
    you will tread our sins underfoot
    and hurl all our iniquities into the depths of the sea.
    (Mic. 7:18–19)

SOUL CARE PRACTICE NO. 4

Give and receive grace generously.

Be Radically Honest with Yourself

1. When have you screwed up and desperately longed for grace?

2. Think of a time you have forgiven someone graciously. How did it leave you feeling?

3. Who have you withheld forgiveness from?

4. How can you show "I love you more than ____," and with whom do you most need to practice living that out?

5. How do you pursue healthy, productive conflict instead of succumbing to cancel culture?

CHAPTER 5

You Are Not the Only One

The best part of parenthood is when the kids go to sleep. OK, I'm only half-joking about that. Really though, Eric and I have our best conversations when the kids have gone down for the night. The same is true whenever we're visiting friends who have children. We can hang out all evening catching up and having a good time despite the million interruptions kids bring to a gathering, but we rarely get into anything serious or meaningful until the children are sleeping and the adults can be fully present.

I recall this distinct transition vividly from a recent time Eric and I were visiting some out-of-state friends. We were having a ball, laughing and eating together. If you would've asked me how they were doing, I would have replied "Amazing!" with full confidence. I mean, they were slaying parenting, and in their home joy abounded. So, after they'd put their kids to sleep and we'd opened a bottle of wine, you can imagine the shock on my face as they sat on opposite ends of the couch, slowly sipping, and disclosed the fact that they were contemplating a separation and divorce. Infidelity had slithered its way into their marriage. I remember wanting to leap out of my seat as I fought back tears. *Don't do it!* I thought. While Eric and I weren't ready in that moment to disclose our past struggles and all we'd overcome, I appreciated the fact that this couple let us in on their reality. You see, up until then, I'd never met anyone else who had anything even remotely similar happen in their marriage. I'd heard of it, of course, but because everyone I knew and did life with didn't fall into that camp, I often felt alone in my weakness.

Lucky for me, these friends of ours went first. They didn't try to impress us. They invited us into their darkness and gave us an opportunity to look for the lamps. With bits of encouragement and deeply raw conversation, we found them and flipped the switch. Grace and peace began illuminating the darkness; our friends found a sliver of hope for healing and restoration.

Since then, Eric and I have had the opportunity to lead the way by going first for others. Every time we let someone in on the hardest part of our marriage and my personal rock bottom, we are humbled. I've learned that when you come out of hiding, you discover so many people, even in your inner circle, who have struggled with the same sin as you. Instead of feeling embarrassed, you realize you are not the only one, which in itself is a flicker of light in the darkness.

You Cannot Heal in Hiding

We all hide things we have yet to heal. Maybe for you it's hiding your lack of sleep by gulping an unspoken amount of caffeine throughout the workday. Perhaps you hide your mess by shoving junk into drawers. Or maybe you hide unhappiness by acting excessively cheerful. A lot of people I know attempt to hide weight gain by wearing loose-fitting, all-black clothes. Some of us hide deep fears and insecurity by habitually overcommitting and overpromising.

Sadly, a lot of us live so focused on hiding parts of ourselves—the parts that society deems weak, embarrassing, or unimpressive— that we never do the real work necessary for healing. Every day, we attempt to hide broken pieces of our spirits and keep hidden the wounds of our souls. However, living in hiding is so much more exhausting than the healing we place on the back burner.

I remember when I finally accepted that I needed help. Beyond that, I remember when I desperately needed hope. I could get neither help nor hope by hiding my sin and struggles. I had to come out of hiding and acknowledge that my life and my very orchestrated, protected persona were a scam. If I wanted to heal once and for all, I had to come out of hiding. I had to be known and seen in full, for the very first time.

One of the most healing seasons in my life was when I first came out of hiding. When I stepped forward to admit that I needed help, I began to feel free. As I announced to myself and a few trusted friends that I needed support, I instantly felt relief run through my veins. You see, just admitting I wasn't OK and coming clean made me feel empowered instead of helpless. My admission opened the door to recovery, and I thankfully was able to reclaim my life.

Knowing what I know now, I'd do it all again in a heartbeat—even though it's awkward, painful, and hard. If you are hurting, exhausted, or living in fear, I believe the path forward is to come out of hiding. Even if you have to do it slowly, come out and speak to someone you trust! The only way you'll ever be fully loved is if you're fully known. Confessing our mess and surrendering are worth it; we just can't do it on our own.

I don't know what you are hiding or keep hidden from your past. Maybe you don't know how to stop gossiping, or you've swiped your card till you're in an embarrassing amount of debt. Perhaps you have a pornography addiction or anger to the point of rage. Your hidden struggles might have to do with lust, alcohol, pride, self-harm, stealing, or lying. Or it might be none of those things. Maybe you think this book isn't for you because your sin isn't that "big" or serious, but I am telling you that this is precisely what the Enemy wants us to think—that our junk isn't a huge deal. Maybe for you it's thinking pridefully, telling a white lie, judging someone online, or overeating, just to name a few. Over time, just like it happened in my own life, our boundary lines get fuzzier and our sin is no longer a gnat we can swat away but a beast we become owned by. Before we know it, we're entangled when we could've been set free.

You can't heal what you hide, but whatever you are willing to reveal, God can heal.

What Living Hidden Steals from You

Whenever I received a compliment during the time in my life when I was hiding and ashamed, I'd negate it in my mind, thinking *If only they knew*. It didn't matter if the compliment was about my ability to speak up in a meeting or how great a friend I was. Even if those things were true, I couldn't receive the praise. I was swallowed up in self-deprecation because of the secret sin and shame I carried.

Now, as I live in the light and pursue inner health each day, I know that we can be right in the midst of a relapse or struggle of some sort and still be good. Receiving praise isn't reserved for perfect people. It wasn't until after my experience of coming clean and working through my sin tangibly that I began to recognize any good within my soul.

Living in hiding steals your ability to connect and to receive praise and steals your last shred of confidence. Living in hiding takes a lot of things from you, but none are worse thefts than the ability to be in authentic relationship with others. Ironically, the very things I kept hidden from people in fear that they wouldn't love me if they knew were the things that made them love me more once they knew. As transparency made its way into my days and my friends didn't run in the opposite direction upon realizing that I was as flawed as they come, I was able to believe and to take back what had been stolen from me. I was able to reclaim my life.

We can live embarrassed because of our junk or confident because of God's grace. Having tried both, I recommend the latter. In her first book, *If You Only Knew*, Jamie Ivey says, "When we hide the mess we've been through, we also hide the redemption that God has lavishly poured on us. We can't proclaim His grace until we expose our mess."[1]

Truth Trumps Feelings

The year 2020 brought enormous changes to the world, including wearing masks to help prevent the spread of COVID-19. But long before 2020, I, along with many people, already wore a mask. Only these masks aren't visible to anyone else. Worn to hide parts of ourselves we're ashamed of or to pretend we're someone entirely different, these masks leave us feeling like a phony.

While hiding behind my own mask, I felt like a fraud. But after I made my confession, I felt relief. Later, on the path of healing and recovery, I felt lighter. Today, I am free.

The work is ongoing. We will never be finished. We will never not have a shadow that lurks in the dark, because sin entered this world. But God is forever in the business of restoration. We do not have to live fake and ashamed. There is a way—even after our worst and most embarrassing struggles are revealed and we stand fully exposed in the light—to move forward in confidence.

First, we must acknowledge and believe that we are not alone in the mistakes we've made and the sin we struggle with. To do this, we have to be willing to go first. To open up and trust that on the other side we will find others who relate in their own way. We will soon discover that we are not monsters.

Second, we must squash shame over and over again. Shame will steal our joy and shut us out until we are isolated. We combat this by embracing who we are—all of who we are, including our insecurities and triggers—rather than striving to fulfill an outside notion of who we think we should be.

Finally, we have to take God's Word over the critiques in our minds or the feelings that will swallow us up if we don't keep them in check.

While we were in premarital counseling, Aaron, our friend who happens to be a pastor, said, "Eric and Manda, there will be times in your marriage where you become upset with each other. It will be your responsibility to say to yourself in those moments: I feel X, but I know Y. It will be one of the hardest things to do in the heat of the moment, but if you can be so disciplined as to replace your feelings with truth, it will serve you well for the long haul."

We have only been married for seven years, but I can tell you that advice has served us well. Just a few weeks ago, I grew annoyed with Eric for goofing around when I was trying to address some serious concerns about our children with him. I felt disrespected in that conversation, even if it wasn't his intention. To approach this in a way that was productive, I had to first remind myself of what Aaron said: *I feel X, but I know Y.* In this case, *I feel disrespected, but I know my husband was just being playful, not malicious.* Separating our feelings from the truth is important for the health of our marriage.

In fact, this piece of wisdom from premarital counseling is what I credit for our recovery and restoration being much smoother than one would imagine. As I continue to let Eric in on my once-secret struggle of longing to be desired by men, he is discouraged and frustrated. Who wants a spouse with *that* struggle, of all things? However, his response in the moments, days, months, and years has always been: *I feel X, but I know Y.* In this case, *I feel disappointed, but I know Manda loves me, and, by choosing to let me in, she is showing that love in the most intimate way possible.*

Feelings Are Meant to Report to Us, Not Rule Us

Our feelings are valid. We should pay attention to them. They serve a purpose. However, that purpose is not to run our lives.

Imagine, for a moment, a life where your feelings are in the driver's seat. I'll use my own feelings for examples: *I feel tired from binge-watching Netflix last night, so I'll just skip work today. I feel left out by my friends, so I'll just get new ones. I feel unloved by my husband, so I'll find fulfillment in the arms of another man.* While some of these examples are obviously more extreme than others, they are all problematic. When we allow feelings to steer our actions, we take a very dangerous path.

On the flip side, here's what it would look like for truth to trump my feelings: *I feel tired from binge-watching Netflix last night, so I will set stricter limits around my TV time in order to get the sleep I need. I feel left out by my friends, so I will have a conversation with them to address it. I feel unloved by my husband, so tonight I will initiate a discussion with him in which we identify ways to speak each other's love languages more intentionally.*

Notice the difference? When our feelings rule us, we make irrational, impulsive, and immature decisions, using emotion to justify our behavior. But when our truth trumps our feelings, we become owners who can rationally identify a healthy next step.

Confidence Boosters

There were numerous moments of breakthrough throughout my inner healing journey after I made my confession. First, I realized I wasn't alone in my struggles. Next, I was no longer buried in shame and felt free. Then I replaced a victim mindset with total ownership. Finally, God provided people who taught me how to rebuild my confidence.

Everything Is an Experiment

A former boss of mine, Kelly, the executive pastor at the church I used to work for, introduced me to a concept that has remained a practice in my life years later. One day she brought me into her office and told me I was doing a wonderful job in my role, but that I was not there to maintain and coast; rather, I was there to innovate and improve. She did not believe in the saying, "If it's not broken, don't fix it." In fact, she wanted me to take some risks and shake things up even though nothing needed fixing. Her antidote for complacency and stagnancy was to have her team create and execute experiments.

I came up with a few things, nothing too risky at first. I experimented with how we might connect with more people by shifting our welcome desk to the first-floor lobby. I thought, *What's the worst thing that could happen? We don't, and then we simply move the desk back to where it has always been.*

Kelly soon challenged me to take it a step further, explaining, "I want you to experiment with something that could actually embarrass you if it doesn't go well." She assured me there would be no judgment or consequences if the experiment failed. The worst thing that could happen was me feeling embarrassed.

So I tried some higher-risk experiments. Things such as putting all of our hosts (the people who help seat you at church) on headsets so I could communicate with them from the balcony, having a brunch for newcomers where they could ask anything they wanted, and purchasing wagons for our street team volunteers to help families by wheeling their children inside. Some were a flop and others made sense to continue doing.

As strange as it was, I learned so much through the practice of experimenting often. What was not working found a new way to work, and what was already good became better. Viewing everything as an experiment took the pressure off and unleashed new creativity in me.

I also took this into my personal life and challenged myself to experiment in healthy ways. I began to step out of my comfort zone as often as possible and just see what happened. The result was a growing confidence that I could do hard things—and the world wouldn't stop spinning when I fell on my face.

Prepare to Fall on Your Face

While my confidence grew to a place where I knew I'd recover from falling on my face, I also learned that it wasn't a matter of *if*

I'd fall, but *when*. When we recognize that we are imperfect people and cannot obtain perfection, we can say adios to all the striving and pretending. We can live so freely that we put ourselves out there, at risk for humiliation . . . or genius.

Liz Bohannon, author and CEO of a global company, decided to go for a crazy idea she had right before a big conference. She thought it would be unique and impactful to "fly" offstage after speaking to thousands, so she brought the idea to the event organizers, and they made a way for her to do just that. She was harnessed and attached to cables in order to fly high above the crowd as the exit from her inspiring talk.[2] This would be viewed as either a bust *or* the perfect way to go out with a bang. Her unique and fun idea could've gone either way with the audience, but wouldn't you know? It was a huge hit! Her experiment in taking the risk probably felt awkward and silly, but I'm sure she has no regrets. Because of her willingness to potentially embarrass herself, she gained thousands of presale orders for her new book. The risk was worth the reward.

My friend Jenna really wanted to find a life partner but was determined to meet him the "old-fashioned" way. However, after my incessant nagging, she finally created an online dating profile because I convinced her it would be a just-for-fun experiment. She ended up marrying the very first guy she connected with on the very app she had poked fun at for so long! Some experiments truly change our lives forever.

Since I have one trillion thoughts per day and some strong opinions, I'd always wanted to create a podcast. But I told myself it wasn't worth it because "everyone" was already doing it. I believed there wasn't room for me in an overly saturated market. Then, one day, it dawned on me: I could create a podcast purely as an experiment. This relieved me of the self-induced pressure I was feeling to make a podcast that topped the charts. At first, *A Longer Table Podcast* was made up of solo episodes. Then it evolved into brief conversations with various guests. It continues to evolve day by day, but the truth is, I don't have a plan. I'm just taking it one experiment at a time, pivoting as I go. It's been super fun and relaxing to approach it this way rather than laboring to make a very rigid vision work.

But let's be honest, not every experiment is going to be a hit. Not every decision we make is going to please everyone. We need to prepare for the fall, expecting it to happen. We will inevitably face rejection, insecurity, and criticism. Instead of waiting for it to happen and trying to deal in the midst of our feelings, I've found it most helpful to be prepared. Before putting myself out there, taking a risk, or executing an experiment in my personal or professional life, I do the following:

1. I question my motives to be fully aware of my "why" and avoid unnecessary embarrassment.
2. I ensure that the people I'm going to share this moment with are the right ones.
3. I picture the absolute worst response I could get. (Seriously, once you picture the *worst*, you realize anything else is going to be cherry pie.)
4. I repeat affirmations, including, "I am who God says I am. My identity is completely separate from this."

I don't care how awful your past is or how embarrassing your present may be. If we were sitting across from each other right now, there's not a thing you could say that would shock me. What matters even more than my opinion is God's. I know beyond a shadow of a doubt that God knows you and already declares you *good*. You aren't stuck. You don't have to repeat cycles of sin and struggle. You can become new right now, at this very moment. Don't wait for the stars to align. Come out of hiding. Rip off your mask. Remind yourself of truth when your feelings creep up. Embrace embarrassment and experiment often. Your life is too valuable to be spent in hiding. You're not the only one who struggles in the ways that you do.

Someone else needs to know they are not alone. Are you willing to go first?

[Be] confident of this, that he who began a good work in you will carry it on to completion until the day of Christ Jesus. (Phil. 1:6)

SOUL CARE PRACTICE NO. 5
Embrace embarrassment for the sake of freedom.

Be Radically Honest with Yourself

1. What is something you have felt embarrassed about, and why?
2. What is a struggle you have, and how could you use it for good?
3. What are three positive qualities you possess?
4. Do your feelings rule you or report to you, and why?
5. What's one experiment you could implement to spark confidence?

CHAPTER 6

Impressing Is Exhausting

When I first came up with the mantra "Impressing is exhausting," everyone I shared it with nodded in agreement. We found solidarity in our weariness of trying to appear better than we actually were. We were worn out and desperate for whatever might be on the other side.

Sadly, many people mistook "Impressing is exhausting" for a surface-level, trendy phrase without real significance. I was constantly tagged in photos and captions using the hashtag that felt superficial. Its watered-down definition lured women to post makeup-less selfies. While I appreciated those women were trying to "keep it real," I feared the much deeper meaning was getting missed.

"Impressing is exhausting" is about a much deeper struggle we all face—the scuffle within our souls.

Maybe when you think of "impressing," your mind goes back to that annoying girl from college who always had to be perfectly dolled up, bragged about herself incessantly, and, without fail, found ways to flaunt her money, status, charitable contributions, or whatever would please the crowd most.

Sometimes, that's what we do when we impress. We put on a façade of sorts, maybe "showing off." But that's not the only way to impress. Sometimes our impressing looks like the complete opposite and no one, except for ourselves, would even recognize we're doing it. This kind of impressing is when we alter ourselves to hide parts of ourselves.

Personally, I've done both. I've shown off, which comes from a place of insecurity—believing I'm not enough and must prove my worth. I've also hidden, which comes from a place of insecurity as well as from the belief that I am too much and will not be accepted as I am.

The night before last Thanksgiving, my husband and I were back in his hometown. We met up with a bunch of his friends and their spouses at a restaurant to catch up over drinks and appetizers. Since we lived in Chicago, a few hours away, it was a treat to get face-to-face time with these friends. As if we were still in middle school, the tables were split by gender. The men corralled to one side of the table to talk about sports and heaven only knows what else while the women stuck together on the other side chatting about our kids, the latest workouts we'd been into, and which contestant we hoped would win on *The Bachelor*.

During this particular evening, I was seated at the corner of a table by a wife I didn't know super well, Claire. Eric and I had attended their wedding a couple of years after our own, and I knew they had just had their second baby, but aside from her marital status and how many children she had, I didn't know her very well. I was eager to hear about her passions and learn what she was like.

We sipped our margaritas, dunked our chips in salsa, and started twenty-seven conversations at once. Claire and I were soon in our own little conversation, and she began telling me that the day she had her second baby was the worst day of her life. As I listened and asked questions, trying to understand how that could be, I grew increasingly perplexed. She and her husband conceived both of their children on the first try, and she'd had two smooth pregnancies and complication-free deliveries. Her older son, now a toddler, was perfectly healthy and had slept through the night since the day they brought him home, according to her. Claire then explained that the technician misread the ultrasound for her second baby, so while she planned and prepared for another baby boy, she was utterly shocked when she gave birth to a perfectly healthy and beautiful baby girl instead. Looking into my eyes, she admitted, "That's why it was the worst day of my life. I had to grieve the loss of my baby boy and find it in my heart to love this little girl I wasn't expecting or prepared for."

At that moment, the Spirit of God stirred something within me that I could not contain. Despite not having a longstanding history of friendship with her, I put my hand on Claire's shoulder and spoke the truth in love. "If that is the worst day of your life, you have a pretty freaking amazing life."

Now, I'm not saying we shouldn't make space to grieve the picture we had in our minds of what would be. I mean, we're all grieving shattered expectations and hopes we had that never got met, aren't we? But as soon as the words came out of my lips, Claire's eyes widened, and she looked like I'd just punched her in the gut. I immediately felt insecure about what I'd said, even though I meant it.

Later that evening, though, a few other women approached me privately to thank me for being courageous enough to say what they had been thinking and gossiping about behind Claire's back. One woman in particular, who had faced multiple miscarriages, told me that it had been so hard hearing her tell that story repeatedly, because she had no idea what it was like to try for seven years to conceive—only to leave the hospital empty-handed.

Even though I received this affirmation, I went to bed wondering why it had to be me. *Why did I speak so bluntly? Why couldn't someone else have said it?*

You see, all of my life I've been quieting, suppressing, and shrinking my "too much" personality. I wished away the parts of myself that I had yet to realize God intended for good, things such as being a truth-teller, an advocate, and an authoritative female. Instead, I "impressed," playing the character of a woman whom I thought people would approve of. When I was that version of myself, hidden-Manda, I withheld in an effort to "impress," and it was equally as exhausting as the times I'd been showoff-Manda. Hidden-Manda never would've spoken to Claire like that.

The next morning, I woke up to a private direct message notification. It was Claire. My stomach dropped, because I had a feeling she was going to be upset with me for what I'd said the night before. Much to my surprise, her message was a note of thanks. She said that while my words weren't easy to receive, the Holy Spirit had used me to speak exactly what she needed to hear. She told me it changed her life. She was sincerely grateful.

Tears filled my eyes, and I realized in that very moment that my life was forever changed too. God used this to reveal that he would use me, but not if I'm trying to be someone else. I surrendered. No more impressing. No more showoff-Manda, living exhausted from trying to measure up. No more hidden-Manda, living exhausted from trying to withhold parts of myself.

Life without impressing has been wildly freeing. I truly feel like I've discovered a life hack, and I can't keep it to myself. I want to tell everybody about it. That's why I'm writing this book. I want others to access this freedom, wholeness, security, and healing. I want to use the gifts God has given me to help point others to the light.

While there is nothing wrong with wanting more for your life, going after goals and whatnot, there is nothing that matters more than the condition of your soul.

The Message version of Mark 8:36–37 asks, "What good would it do to get everything you want and lose you, the real you? What could you ever trade your soul for?" I'll answer that question throughout this book over and over again: *nothing*. Nothing is worth gaining at the expense of your soul.

Drop the Act

Have you ever been in the car with your spouse, significant other, or a friend on the way to an event, and they decide it's the perfect time to bring up something like the thing you did yesterday that bothered them?

Eric and I both pick the worst times to fight. It seems like things always pop up when we're running late for a gathering and want to look our best. We somehow manage to get into a disagreement, tensions run high, and we each get in our final words just before slamming the car doors shut.

We were in a juvenile disagreement about who left the box of Cinnamon Toast Crunch cereal out on the counter just as we were headed out for a double date with a couple we'd met at church. We were both dressed to the nines, but neither of us acknowledged it as we normally would because we were too busy making our case against each other about the cereal. By the time we pulled up to the restaurant, our argument had escalated significantly. It was no longer about the cereal but about twenty other things, and our jabs didn't help. Already running late, we had to table the dispute and put our happy faces on. Things were tense as we walked inside and greeted our friends. We avoided eye contact with each other and focused on them. When they asked, "How are you guys?" I wondered if I should say the truth. Instead I blurted, "We're good!" nearly out of habit. We didn't get past small talk before the waiter seated us. I wasn't enjoying myself at all. I looked at Eric, and then it came out, like word vomit.

"So, we were just arguing about who left the Cinnamon Toast Crunch out on the counter before we got here, and that's why there's an unspoken tension between us right now. I'm sorry," I said.

Our friends immediately started laughing. I look over at Eric, who put his hand on my thigh, a sign of assurance that I'd broken the tension by calling out the elephant in the room, which was now shrinking in size.

Maybe it sounds like a small thing: arriving to a double date and surrendering your need to appear perfect in order to acknowledge the truth that you just got done arguing. It might seem small, but showing up *real* is hard work. It requires us to be vulnerable and courageous. Not only does it benefit us but the people we're with will really appreciate it.

There's no one better to learn from when it comes to vulnerability than one of my favorite authors, Brené Brown. She says, "The willingness to show up changes us, it makes us a little braver each time," and I agree.[1] However, the practice of showing up real feels awkward at first. And as someone who's been working on this intentionally for years, I should warn you: not everyone is going to respond to your real with love or acceptance. Showing up real might scare away a few people you once called friends. Showing up real might upset family members who prefer the shiny, cleaned-up façade you've put on for so long. If showing up real were easy, we'd all do it, and there wouldn't be hundreds of apps available to help us achieve faux perfection in every photo.

Our Longing to Belong

In high school, I wore way too much black eyeliner, tanned excessively, and continuously bleached my hair. I did everything I possibly could to make myself look a certain way on the outside. I wanted to fit in with the cool crowd. Unfortunately for me, I was always in between. I was too interested in Jesus and did not drink, which set me apart from my popular peers, but I was too obvious about my desire to be popular for my classmates on the outskirts. I straddled the line and got hit by both sides of traffic.

While I was able to achieve a certain look on the outside, my attempts to be like those cool kids never quite fooled anyone—including myself. I tried so hard to be someone I wasn't because I didn't accept myself for who I was. Even when I appeared to fit in, I never felt like I belonged.

Looking back to those high school years, and even to last week, I see clearly that so much of my drive to impress is motivated by a desire to belong. The irony is that there is only one way to belong: to accept yourself. It's so stupidly simple that I think we overlook it often. Accepting ourselves as we are, flaws, quirks, and all, is a prerequisite for belonging.

This is why impressing is exhausting. When we live in a state of trying to fit in, to be a little more of this or a little less of that, we reject our true selves; the ones created by God who are the culmination of our biological makeup, nurturing experiences, and nature's course. When we reject our true selves, we impress and present a falsified version of ourselves to the world, hoping that when someone accepts us we'll feel better. The problem is that even when we're accepted, it's inauthentic. It might feel good for a moment, but we never truly belong.

I couldn't possibly recount all of the times in my life I've decided I was just going to fake it till I made it; there are far too many. Cheerleading tryouts in high school, job interviews after college, and relationships along the way. The biggest lesson I've learned: you won't make it very far if you aren't free, and you aren't free if you're faking it.

We can try to fool ourselves into thinking we don't need anybody, but the truth is we are hardwired for community. We were made for each other, and that's why a life of faking it always leaves us feeling lonelier than ever.

No Freedom in Faking It

Even though I'd like to believe I haven't been a liar since middle school, I caught myself lying at a gathering in Los Angeles just a few years ago. Eric and I were there with a bunch of people whom I perceived to be far more accomplished and therefore "above" me. At first, I coped by just keeping the conversation focused on them. I got them talking about themselves and kept them there. I didn't want to talk about what I did or who I was because I felt embarrassed. *Hi, I write a blog and it's tiny. No, you haven't heard of it because I'm literally a blip on the radar. You just curated the music for that movie with Leonardo DiCaprio? Sweet. I'm way out of my league here.* But inevitably, the conversation turned to me, and the words that poured out of my mouth were fabrications of the truth. Eric was flabbergasted as he heard me. As soon as there was a break in the conversation, he lovingly pulled me aside. "Babe, why did you make it seem like you were speaking to a much bigger audience at your latest event? Why were you stretching the truth?"

With tears in my eyes, I told him I wasn't sure why I was fabricating, but that I needed to pull myself together. I went off to the restroom and stood in a stall for a few minutes. While taking deep breaths, I closed my eyes and brought myself in tune with the present moment. I got honest with myself about what was going on. I was trying to impress these people because I wanted to belong. However, it was backfiring. You can't really belong when you aren't being real. I wanted to rush out the door and speed home to hide under my covers forever. I felt like a fool. Then, it dawned on me. *What if I just walk back over to them and apologize for not being truthful? What if I admit how out of place I feel and just own it?* Before I could talk myself out of it, that's exactly what I did.

I approached the small circle we'd been mingling with for most of the night. Eric was still with them. I sheepishly interrupted them and said something along the lines of, "Well, this is awkward, but I've been really intimidated by you all tonight and it's made me act a lot different from who I really am. My blog is small, and I really am more in the Christian niche of writers. I'm proud of what I get to spend my days doing, but by no means am I speaking to thousands. Most of my events only have about fifty people, tops. I'm sorry I wasn't entirely truthful. I feel so embarrassed."

You know what I was met with? Enormous kindness and positivity. These people assured me that I didn't need to be anything more, less, or different from who I was. They ended up asking me a ton of questions about my work and passions. It led to a beautiful conversation, connections, and talk of how we could partner in the future. Initially, I didn't feel like I belonged only because I wasn't free. We can never be free when we're faking it.

Wisdom Withholds

A few nights after moving into our new home, we put the boys to bed and had a few of our closest friends over, two couples, to celebrate the move and all the hopes we had for the memories we would make in our new space. The guys made their way downstairs with a bag of Doritos and got comfortable on the couch so they could keep an eye on the big screen, where the game was on. On the other hand, we girls sat around my candlelit kitchen table with some sea salt dark chocolate to pair with our red wine. It was the perfect setting for a fun and meaningful evening, until without much warning one of my friends burst into tears, spilling the tea about how much her marriage was in shambles. She didn't give many details, maybe out of respect for their relationship or because her husband was just one floor below us, still in earshot. Regardless, our other girlfriend and I didn't press her for information. We mostly listened, asked questions from a place of curiosity, offered encouragement, and asked how we could best be there for them during this difficult time. What transpired next really caught me off guard.

She pivoted the conversation abruptly, asking me to *just tell her already* about what happened in my marriage early on. She'd picked up on bits and pieces from things I'd alluded to in conversation and in my writing. She explained that she knew something bad must have happened, and if we were truly best friends, I wouldn't keep anything from her.

I was not prepared for this. Sharing something so major, even though it happened years ago—something my marriage had recovered from but would also be forever healing in many ways—is really vulnerable and should be done on my own terms, according to our therapist. Yet here I was, being pressured into sharing more than I was ready to share. I tried to explain that, out of respect for my own marriage, I didn't feel comfortable getting into it right then, but she pushed and got very emotional. She asked me questions relentlessly and manipulated me until she got more information than I was interested in sharing. Still not satisfied, she accused me of not being transparent and mocked me for claiming to be authentic. I felt so misunderstood. I wasn't trying to be fake whatsoever; I just wasn't ready to expose all our scars. Although she didn't get everything, I still felt robbed.

I walked away from that evening believing more than ever before that there is wisdom in withholding, and that being authentic doesn't mean sharing flippantly. I knew deep in my bones that I'd been authentic and genuine. I knew that my choice not to share everything with her hadn't been motivated by the need to impress but rather came from a place of wisdom.

I think one of the biggest misconceptions today is associating authenticity with how much or little we share with others. We're confusing authenticity with transparency. We write people off and attach labels like *fake* or *inauthentic* when we couldn't possibly know what's going on inside their souls. Maybe they aren't sharing about something because they aren't ready, or you simply aren't someone they have chosen to hold space for them. Wisdom withholds for the right person, place, and time.

Prone to Pretend

The Enneagram, as I mentioned in chapter 2, has been trending for a while now, and sadly it's often misused. Many people think it's a personality test, similar to the Myers-Briggs, but it's better understood as a powerful and insightful tool for understanding ourselves and others. The Enneagram can help us see ourselves at a deeper, more objective level, and can be of invaluable assistance in our path to self-knowledge and awareness. Personally, I'm a huge Enneagram fan because it addresses the motivation behind a person's actions rather than the action itself.

After taking the test and doing your own research, you will identify as one of the nine different types: Reformer (1), Helper (2), Achiever (3), Individualist (4), Investigator (5), Loyalist (6), Enthusiast (7), Challenger (8), or Peacemaker (9).[2] Upon discovering that I most resonate with type 8, I began to notice moments where I was acting from a need or desire to control. As I learned this about myself and read up on the healthy and unhealthy parts of my type through books such as *The Road Back to You* and *Sacred Enneagram*, I was able to notice and thereby resist some of my unhealthy tendencies and also implement practices that would serve my soul and the people around me. Things like practicing mercy, allowing someone else to take the lead, owning my emotional needs, and not seeking out confrontation. This is why, yet again, awareness is the first prerequisite for transformation. We cannot change what we aren't aware of.

I think Enneagram 3s get a bad rap because although they are called "the Achiever," there is a lot of supporting text about how image-conscious they are. In fact, one of their key motivations is to impress people. For about ten seconds, I thought I might be a type 3. After all, I've always been a high achiever and have struggled with trying to impress others throughout my life. However, the basic fears and desires of type 3 didn't resonate at all, and the test confirmed my suspicions that I was, in fact, much more of a type 8, the Challenger. This is why it's crucial, if you're going to utilize the Enneagram as a tool in your life, to really dig deep.

I hate to break it to you, but trying to impress and performing, especially in social settings, isn't reserved for Enneagram 3s. I'm convinced we are all performers at one time or another. I mean, how could we not be? We live in a time when, thanks to ever-evolving technology, we have the ability to create whatever persona we want, most often our ideal self. We view accomplishments and productivity as more important than relationships, especially in this country. I'll never forget the distinct difference I noticed when I lived overseas.

As an aspiring elementary school teacher, when I was studying to earn my bachelor's in education, I seized the opportunity to complete my student teaching in a fourth-grade classroom in the beautiful country of Costa Rica. At first, I absolutely loved it there. The weather, the friendly people, the way the whole place felt like a beach town even though I was inland. But it didn't take long for me to grow impatient and frustrated with the slow pace of life. If my host family drove us somewhere, it took everything in me not to ask why we couldn't step on it a bit more. If my students came to class tardy, there were no consequences. After school every day, I was invited to join the other teachers as they gathered in the teachers' lounge, bringing pan, chicharrones, and café, of course. Unlike me, they weren't in a hurry to leave. While I thought about how I needed to grade papers, finish lesson plans, squeeze in a workout, and finish a book I was reading in order to hit my goal for the year, they were not concerned about anything but "wasting time" together. Developing deeper friendships and investing time into one another, they weren't actually wasting time. Whenever I chose to stay and returned home later than usual, my host mom would greet me by saying, "*Estoy muy orgullosa de ti por perder el tiempo hoy, Amanda,*" which means, "I'm so proud of you for wasting time today." She had hosted many Americans before and confided in me that she felt sorry for us. She expressed how terrible it must be to live like "that," referring to our busy, overstuffed, productive lives that often lacked relational depth. The lessons I learned there are invaluable. Since then, I've focused more on people than productivity and in taking an interest in others more than impressing them.

Three Ways to Stop Pretending

Every single one of us is prone to pretending at times, but if we want to live more meaningful lives that aren't exhausting and instead have an ease and lightness to them, we must check our motives, pursue wholeness, and get accountable.

Check Your Motives

In everything you say, do, share online, and stay silent about, it's helpful to dig deep and ask yourself some questions.

- Why? *Why did I say that? Why am I posting this? Why didn't I speak up?*
- What is my intention? *What am I trying to accomplish by taking this course of action?*
- Is there anything driving me that shouldn't be? *Fear, the need to prove my worth, an attempt to avoid conflict?*

You can't control how people perceive you, so don't waste your time. However, you can control how you live your life, so check your motives to ensure you're operating from a place of sincerity, love, and wholeness.

Pursue Wholeness

In my younger days, I was a competitive gymnast. I could still practice when my leotard became worn and faded from the ongoing wear, sweat, and wash cycle. I could still perform if the curls in my hair fell flat the morning of a competition. I could still compete even if one of my teammates didn't show up. The one absolute necessity to compete in my sport was a healthy body.

I worked hard to take care of it, prevent injuries, and nurture it with the right foods. Getting adequate sleep was nonnegotiable, and ice baths were a regular occurrence. Occasionally, my mom spoiled me with a deep-tissue massage at the spa. I showed abundant love and care to my body, because without it I couldn't do what I loved most: be a gymnast. Long before crushes on boys, gymnastics was my obsession. When I neglected to care for my body properly, I grew fatigued and got injured, and my scores at meets reflected it. Without tremendous care for their physical health, gymnasts suffer immensely.

You may have never cared much for gymnastics, but the point is this: we all have a body that needs proper care in order to do what we love most. Without proper care, whatever we have devoted our lives to will suffer. Maybe you are currently studying your way through college or working full-time. Maybe you're a spouse, parent, business owner, or all of the above. Your body lets you know when it needs some extra attention, right? Your eye twitches when you're stressed and not getting enough sleep. Your back starts to ache if you're sitting at a desk hunched over for too long or holding a baby with horrible posture for hours because it's the only way she'll sleep. You get a headache if you skip meals or don't drink water throughout the day. Our bodies give signals.

Similarly, our souls send us signals when we aren't taking care of them. These signals, often overlooked and even avoided, are known only to you because they are completely unseen by others. They look like jealousy, avoidance, faking it, envy, negative thoughts, ill will toward others, and more.

If we don't want to go through life pretending, we must tend to our souls and pursue wholeness. Pursuing wholeness looks different for everyone, because we're all different people with different needs and personalities. Here are twenty ways I pursue wholeness:

1. Confess—your greatest sin and struggles lose their power when you name them aloud.

2. Read—to learn, ponder, reflect, and grow.

3. Unplug—in a world that is connected 24/7, go off the grid to find yourself again.

4. Set intentions unrelated to achievements—goals are great, but life isn't all about what you can achieve, so set intentions for how you want to live, not perform.

5. Spend time in solitude—you can't deal with what you won't face.
6. Purge often—toxic relationships, habits, bitterness, grudges, temptations, and so forth.
7. Find a true hobby—do something you love for unadulterated fun without the pressure to monetize or perfect it.
8. Check in instead of numbing out—when your feelings tell you to eat the whole tub of raw cookie dough while binge-watching Netflix, choose to check in on your soul instead through therapy, journaling, or a walk outside.
9. Be spontaneous—in a world full of scheduling, make space for spontaneity and your soul will thank you.
10. Continually reevaluate—What matters to you? What do you value most? What do you want to be remembered for?
11. Admit faults, apologize, and ask forgiveness—humility is a breeding ground for growth.
12. Say no—say no a lot more than you want, because you have limited capacity, and that's not something to fight but rather embrace.
13. Live generously—true generosity requires sacrifice, otherwise it's just being nice. Your soul will shift as you give expecting nothing in return.
14. Release the need to know and control—this is easier said than done, but focus on living with a hands-open posture.
15. Don't skimp on sleep—your body, mind, and soul need it, which is why God created us to do it every single night.
16. Focus inward—whenever things or other people bother you, ask, "What does this say about me?" and allow them to be a mirror for you.
17. Rest—you weren't created to be a human doing. You're a human being.
18. Pray—because even if it doesn't change anything, it will change you.

19. Pay attention—and be mindful of what you're looking for. If you look for the good, you'll find it. If you look for the bad, it's all you'll see.

20. Embrace complexity—we all lead densely layered lives. You, your neighbor, your friend, and the grocery store clerk. Don't view anyone or anything through a black-and-white lens. Don't judge based on one interaction. Hold mixed feelings and things that seem contrary to one another without needing to fully understand.

Which of these do you practice already? Which might you begin to incorporate in your life? How would pursuing wholeness help you to take off your mask when you're most tempted to wear one?

Get Accountable

As with any real and lasting transformation, we won't change overnight and stay that way forever. None of us wake up confident and remain so for all our days. We have to make ongoing decisions to build our confidence. Similarly, we can decide right now that we're done pretending our way through life, but tomorrow will tempt us, and only by God's grace and ongoing practices can we conquer old habits and live in a rhythm of real. This is where accountability comes in!

Do you have people in your corner who love you and have your best interest at heart? Are you willing to be vulnerable with them and ask if they will call you out whenever you're not being real? This is just one option for getting accountability fast. Two additional ways would be to seek out a mentor who can help you grow into your full, authentic self and to set up a schedule to check in with yourself daily or weekly to assess your behavior.

I have one mentor who checks in on me spiritually every week, a different mentor who checks in on how I'm doing when it comes to my heart (and not seeking fulfillment from men) at least once each month, and a counselor who regularly asks me questions about all of the areas in which I am prone to wander down the wrong path. Most recently, I hired a business coach who is providing me with accountability around prioritizing my husband and our boys above my work. All of their accountability comes in the form of asking me black-and-white, factual questions. Outside of this incredible, God-sent team, I also hold myself accountable.

I have a time limit set for my Instagram so I do not scroll aimlessly and waste hours observing the lives of others. I have a reminder that pops up on my phone to see if I've gotten three high-intensity workouts in that week. I am responsible for making to-do lists to get my work done, and I'm responsible for redirecting my thoughts when they go to dark places such as judgment or jealousy. As you may have picked up on already, self-accountability is essential, but it's not enough. That's why I'm so passionate about accountability partners such as mentors, coaches, and trusted friends. They require us to answer to someone other than ourselves.

I believe accountability is a key that can unlock doors of opportunity and healing in your life. But accountability is useless if you don't show up honestly. No more faking it till you've made it; *face it* till you've made it. And you can be sure making it looks a lot more like freedom in Jesus than anything this world puts on a pedestal.

Since God has so generously let us in on what he is doing, we're not about to throw up our hands and walk off the job just because we run into occasional hard times. We refuse to wear masks and play games. We don't maneuver and manipulate behind the scenes. And we don't twist God's Word to suit ourselves. Rather, we keep everything we do and say out in the open, the whole truth on display, so that those who want to can see and judge for themselves in the presence of God. (2 Cor. 4:1–2 Message)

SOUL CARE PRACTICE NO. 6
Live in a rhythm of real.

Be Radically Honest with Yourself

1. When have you longed for acceptance that led you to be someone you're not?
2. In what area(s) of your life are you most prone to pretend?
3. Which soul-tending exercises do you want to start incorporating into your days?
4. Do you struggle to show up *real* online?
5. Describe your real, authentic self. Is there a disconnect in how you portray yourself?

CHAPTER 7

You Are *Already* Good

For the last six years, Eric and I have, with permission, set our friend Greg up on dates. Unfortunately, every single woman comes back to us saying almost the exact same thing. They aren't interested in a second date because, they say, "It feels like he's way more interested in dating himself." Every time we hear this reflection and reasoning, we sigh. We know how much he wants to be in a relationship and find a life partner, but we are painfully aware that he can come across as super self-absorbed.

The truth is that he isn't self-absorbed. What they are seeing are his self-consciousness and insecurity. He talks about himself highly because he feels the need to overcompensate. In reality, he lacks self-esteem, and this gravely holds him back from all God intends for his life. I'm not just talking about finding a life partner, either. We see this holding him back in his work, friendships, spiritual growth, and more. You see, our friend tries extra hard to show parts of himself to people that he thinks they'll approve of as a way to deflect from his flaws or hide the parts of himself he has yet to embrace. He attempts to hide his insecurities by boasting about himself in all the areas he can. To a stranger he's encountering for the first time, he comes across as confident. But in reality, he's super unsure of himself and will say just about anything to convince himself, let alone another person, that he's worthy of love.

Because we've known Greg for years and can see this so clearly, we've never been bothered too much by his bragging moments. We see what's going on below the surface: he fears on a very deep level that he's not good or good enough, and will do anything to convince people around him what he isn't convinced of himself. He might think he does a great job hiding his insecurities, but to everyone who really sees him, they are glaringly on display. For women who are dating to find a spouse, I can completely understand why this is problematic. But let's be honest: it's not only Greg who does this.

We all have subtle ways of compensating for our insecurities when we don't believe we're good or good enough. How often do we text each other to ask, "What are you going to wear?" before a gathering or event? Sometimes, right before I do this, my inner voice reminds me I am more secure than this: *C'mon, Manda, aren't you capable of dressing yourself and rocking it confidently, regardless of what everyone else chooses?*

Insecurity shows up in my life when I really enjoy a book or TV series only to hear that my closest friends say that they thought it was "so lame" or "too dark," and suddenly I'm second-guessing my opinion and changing my mind—at least publicly—just to fit in. Our insecurities also show when we seek advice or vent to nine different people about a decision we're trying to make, and when we get defensive about a small comment that wasn't even intended to be a criticism.

I've noticed a correlation between security and participation when it comes to gossip too. Whether it be starting or spreading it, it's our insecurities that drive this behavior. Secure people don't care about the secret lives of others. Secure people don't want to make other people look bad in order to look good themselves. When we are secure in ourselves, we don't have to sing our own praises to the world. On the other hand, when we are insecure we become so focused on ourselves that we forget to ask others about themselves.

When our beliefs about ourselves come from how we perform and the things others say about us, our sense of self will be ever-changing. We'll spend our days striving to prove to ourselves and everyone around us that we're both good and good enough. As this pressure to prove invades our souls, we become insecure. We turn into self-centered people who are utterly self-conscious. Unless our beliefs about ourselves come from a source that is true, unending, and unchanging, we will always be insecure.

Find Security in the Only One Who Can Provide It

Everything is in a constant state of change. This we know to be true in our own lives, but for a moment I want you to step back and picture it from afar. Think of the world at large. Every single second new babies are born at the same time as other people are taking their last breaths. Australia's winter begins in June as our Midwestern states finally start showing signs of summer. At the very moment you accepted a new job offer, someone else is being told they've been laid off. Someone who's having a bad day can kickstart a ripple effect onto others. Tiny choices in your marriage can lead to big changes "overnight." The same is true for every relationship and job. Your happiest days are someone's worst, and the inverse is also true. There are factors to all of this, of course. Plain old cause and effect is a big one, but also natural disasters and unexplainable unfortunate events are part of reality. With everything and everyone changing every second of the day, I get dizzy just thinking about how scattered and chaotic life truly is.

No wonder we are a hot mess when we try to tap into this life as the source of our security, identity, and purpose. It's all changing at the speed of light! We look for security in our friendships, marriages, jobs, and more. Sometimes we think we've found it for a little while, but no sooner do we relax than we find ourselves back to square one.

Let me be specific here. If your security is found in your job title, then the moment you get demoted you will feel like you failed, and insecurity will come crashing in. If your security is found in your spouse, then the moment he or she makes a decision that hurts you, such as looking at pornography, you are going to feel like you weren't good enough, and insecurity will take over. If your security is found in your material possessions, then you will forever pursue happiness in all the wrong places, and security will become the carrot dangling in front of your nose, always a few inches out of reach.

I see this a lot. People spend their time and energy chasing things they believe will make them good or good enough, or, in other words, secure. They dream of a future that includes larger paychecks, bigger houses, and better wardrobes. They strive and scheme to acquire these things. They go to great lengths to keep up with the Joneses and become jealous when others inch closer to their desired status or have better things. Their security is found in possessions and appearances, which makes it fragile and fleeting at best.

Our hearts and souls know better. They call us back to the importance of things that cannot be seen, purchased, or conjured up through having enough grit. Things like love, hope, integrity, friendship, trust, and compassion. These are the things that bring substance, fulfillment, and lasting joy to our lives. These are the attributes that bring lasting security.

We can seek and pursue security in a million different ways, but there is only One who can provide it: Jesus. When my security is found in him, I'm truly safe because it's real. Everything else is just a false sense of security.

What happens if you spend your entire life finding security in how you look? One day wrinkles will form, and hairs will turn gray. Even though our outer beauty fades, the God of the universe, the most beautiful being, finds us to be beautiful still.

What happens if you spend your life finding security in your physical abilities? One day your legs no longer run as fast as they used to, and your lung capacity is more limited. Even though our bodies wither, God still marvels at us—his creation.

God's love for us never wanes. He doesn't love us less when crow's feet form around our eyes and veins bulge on our calves. He will never love us any more or any less than he does right now. That, my friends, is security.

We are held by the One who holds it all. The knowledge and deep belief in this when everything around us is changing and spinning is *confidence*. When our security is in Jesus, we have confidence in God.

Created in the image and likeness of God, we have an inherent worth. We are "fearfully and wonderfully made," and God's loving thoughts toward us are too numerous to count. God values us so much he sent his Son, Jesus, to die for us so we can be in a close relationship with him. Our security rests in his grace, not our personal merits. This is true, and we have to believe it and marinate in it for our lives to reflect it. Becoming secure in God is a process of learning to rely more and more on the love and grace of God in our lives. Knowing in our heads that God loves us is one thing, but relying on that love is another.

When someone asks me how I can love and then let go of a child we've fostered for a year, I tell them the truth: I trust in God's faithfulness. I genuinely believe he cares about the well-being of these kids even more than me. When someone asks me how I share my life's greatest hardships and most vulnerable moments so publicly, I tell them the truth: I am living for an audience of One. It's easy to share raw, honest moments when my worth is not wrapped up in how people receive or perceive them.

In everything I say and do, I'm fearless because I am rooted in Jesus; he is my source of security. No lifechanging events can rattle this internal rootedness. Security in Jesus cannot be taken from us—unlike every other thing we might try to find our security in.

I dare you to get to a place where what God thinks of you matters more to you than what anyone else thinks. You only get there by practicing daily. I dare you to shift the focus off of yourself and onto him. You and I will always make mistakes and fall short, but if we can focus more on all God does for us rather than if we are enough, we will experience a security that does not waver.

Integrity

Several years ago, a friend of mine became a mother through adoption. I clicked through pictures of her gifts, meals, and visits of people who rallied around her and her new child. While I was happy for her, I felt a twinge of insecurity creep in. *Why didn't I receive a link for the meal train? Are those girls closer to her than I am? Maybe I am a crummy friend.*

I was on a spiral of self-pity. I should have reached out and brought her a meal or a gift. I felt guilty for not doing the good I knew I ought to do. Rather than texting her to congratulate her or sending a Grubhub gift card, I waited on an invitation that never came. It wasn't until later that I found out there had been no invitation. People just did what we should all do in times of major transition: show up. I knew better. It was my lack of integrity that made me feel insecure. These other people had been genuinely good friends to her, and it only bothered me because I knew deep down I could have been a better friend myself. Acknowledging that guilt freed me up to start becoming that kind of friend.

Integrity is a prerequisite for security.

Let me repeat that: integrity is a prerequisite for security.

We can't expect to feel secure in who we are if we're living a lie. When we're hiding something or don't do something we know we're supposed to, we feel terrible and insecure. During the time of my life when I was so entangled in the sin of lust and needing approval from men, I felt insecure about everything. Because I knew what was going on in secret in my own life, I assumed there was something dark going on in my husband's life too. I couldn't possibly trust him. I was too insecure. I was paranoid, searching and looking to catch him. How could I be worthy of anything else? I couldn't give him or my friends—anyone—the benefit of the doubt because here I was, living a double life. My insecurities exhausted me. At the time, my unconfessed sin and shame reinforced the lie that I was not good and could never be good enough.

Security is something we desperately need, and it is something God deeply desires to give us. Searching for it in our job, appearance, or romantic partners will only leave us full of constant worry and envy. Only through a life of integrity can we experience security.

Living as If You're Already Good

Living as if you're already good might seem conceited, but let me set the record straight: when we live like we're already good, it does not mean we are without flaws and shouldn't work on ourselves. It means we function from a deep knowledge that we are good, loved, and worthy—and none of it is by our own doing. When we live from this place, believing we are good because we are made in the image of God and God's innate goodness is within us, it changes everything. No longer are we consumed by other people's opinions of us. No longer are we afraid to chase our dreams and look like a fool if they don't pan out. No longer are we afraid to speak our minds honestly even though someone might disagree. It changes everything because it reduces our fears and enhances our worth. And people who know their worth . . . watch out!

I believe it's the difference between a life lived self-consciously versus *soul*-consciously. When I'm self-conscious, I am me-focused and unaware. I make choices that do not align with what God says about me. On the other hand, when I am soul-conscious, I am deeply aware of the good within me and make choices that agree with God's Word. Both impact everything and everyone around me, but the aftermath is vastly different. It's the difference between what-if and even-if, and the choice to believe bigger is up to us.

Self-conscious living makes decisions out of fear. I can't speak on stage, say "I love you" first, or ask for a promotion because what if I bomb it? What if people talk about me? What if he runs in the other direction? What if they deny my request?

Soul-conscious living makes decisions out of trust. Even if I fail or even if others reject me, I am loved, and my value does not change.

For example, say you consider forgiving someone who hurt you. What-if places power in *their* response. *What if I forgive him and he hurts me again?* But even-if places the power in *your* hands. *Even if I forgive him, and he hurts me again, I will be free because I forgave.* Do you see the direct relationship between what-if and fear, whereas even-if relies on a foundation of trust?

Can you imagine a world full of soul-conscious beings? How drastically different would it look from the world we live in today? How different would our lives be on a personal level? I picture people who don't self-sabotage and who experience breakthroughs in their relationships. I envision wholehearted celebration where now there is often jealousy and comparison. I dream of a world where there is peace and no strife. Maybe soul-conscious living would be heaven in the flesh.

At the root of many of our issues is the belief that we are no good, that we are damaged and unworthy. But if we want our roots to heal, we have to allow Jesus in deep enough. We have to know what we're so desperate to believe: we are already good. And there isn't a single person we wouldn't love if we knew their story. So, the next time you notice someone's arrogance or hear about someone's mistake, remember there's so much more to their story. It is not our job to judge others, and it is not our job to justify our own poor choices. We have one job, and that is to believe we're good not because of how much we get right but simply and only because God is good, and we are made in his image.

You Are Worthy of Every Good Thing

Growing up in a conservative Christian environment, I heard many sermons discouraging me from loving myself or indulging in the things I enjoyed. There were a lot of backhanded compliments in the preaching I heard. Things like, "You are so loved despite all of your brokenness." While this is true, I think sometimes churches and individual Christians focus on all of the ways we fall short instead of simply saying, "You are so loved. Period. Nothing you do or don't do changes that."

Looking back, most of the religion I was taught cultivated a "woe is me" mentality. It was as if being a martyr was the highest calling, and the goal in life was to follow the rules, make no mistakes—and definitely, whatever you do, don't pursue fun. Bonus points if you suffer. I now view this theology as toxic and believe that a God who wants me to suffer is not the God I've grown to know and love.

Eric and I are currently in a period of not accepting any foster children into our home. We have many reasons for this decision, but I'll refrain from sharing those because it isn't the point. In fact, we shouldn't have to justify a decision we feel is best. However, for a while I struggled with feelings of selfishness because the religion I grew up with told me that unless I constantly pursued the hardest life with the most sacrifice and suffering possible, I wasn't following the way of Jesus.

What I've come to know and believe, with every ounce of my being, is that God doesn't want us to pursue a hard life for the sake of struggle. Suffering is bound to happen when we follow Jesus, but it shouldn't be our mission.

God wants us to be happy and delights when we do things that bring true joy to our souls.

For too long, old-school and toxic theology preached that things like having piercings and tattoos, wearing spandex, or drinking alcohol were "of the world" and Christians weren't supposed to

have any part in them. That twisted theology cultivated generations of Christians who were primarily concerned with behavior,
rules, and doing (or not doing) things for all of the wrong reasons.
God cares very little about the petty things we get into Facebook
debates over. I'm pretty sure it's reiterated in the Bible enough
for us to confidently say that God's biggest concern is not if we
enjoy an occasional margarita but rather if we love him and our
neighbors.

He wants you to believe you are good because you are made
in his image. He wants you to live like you believe that instead of
spending your whole life trying to convince yourself and everyone
around you.

The world is best when you are at your best, and that includes
doing things that bring out the goodness in you. Whether it be
sleeping in on Saturdays, hiking in the woods, or going out with
friends—doing what you love matters. It isn't bad or selfish, nor
are you any less of a Christ-follower when you love yourself by
indulging in healthy activities that bring joy to your soul.

If it brings goodness to your soul and to the world, do it unabashedly.

<hr />

I praise you because I am fearfully and wonderfully made;
    your works are wonderful,
    I know that full well. (Ps. 139:14)

SOUL CARE PRACTICE NO. 7

Ground yourself in the good.

Be Radically Honest with Yourself

1. Where are you most tempted to search for security?

2. When do you feel most insecure?

3. Do you believe you are good? Why or why not?

4. What would it look like to live soul-consciously rather than self-consciously?

5. What brings out goodness in you?

CHAPTER 8

Autopilot

I did the whole bounce back and forth between mom and dad's house every other weekend, secretly not wanting to ever leave my mom's. My stepmom, Sharon, treated me like I was there to wait on her hand and foot. She always had me clean and do chores while yelling at me for not doing them up to her standards. She would intimidate me, but instead of lashing out, I made myself smaller. I walked on eggshells, always trying to keep from upsetting her more. Then one Saturday, but not just any Saturday—my seventh birthday, in fact—something tragic happened.

I was at Dad's house because it was his designated weekend, and we were supposed to have a birthday party for me later that evening. My stepmom had given birth to a beautiful baby girl a few months prior, so I had a half-sister named Holly.

The details of this particular day are fuzzy for me, because our brains don't like to remember hard things. Counselors have told me these are called repressed memories. But what I do remember is that early in the afternoon, I was watching *Matilda* on a little TV in my bedroom. Miss Honey was my idol, and I knew I wanted to grow up and be a teacher like her someday, one who cared for students who had abusive caretakers and tough home lives.

My dad and stepmom never got along well, but the new baby made the stress even higher, and things had become even more tense. My birthday party was supposed to start in a few hours, so I tried to just stay out of the way and console Holly whenever she started crying.

I heard Dad and Sharon arguing, which wasn't unusual. This time it was a disagreement in the kitchen about ice cream flavors; something about my dad not picking up the flavors she'd requested. Not long after the words *chocolate* and *strawberry* were shouted came the f-bombs, the slamming of objects, and the sounds of pushing and shoving.

I snuck out of the bedroom quietly to peek around the corner into the kitchen and view round one of their brawl. Scared to death, I watched as the argument escalated by the second. Dad was yelling at the top of his lungs, cursing and stomping. Sharon was screaming back, swearing and slapping. Then came round two: punching, scratching, and tumbling into the living room.

Everything happened so quickly. I don't think either of them could see anything but red and rage. As Dad and Sharon whaled on each other, one of them fell into the glass coffee table, shattering it. Little glass particles flew all over the room like snow.

I cried and screamed, trying to match their volume, begging them to stop. I was horrified.

I saw Holly in her little bouncy seat across the living room, not far from the war taking place before my eyes. I dodged the two of them as they continued into rounds three and four as they rolled on the floor. I got to Holly and scooped her up, then slipped back to my bedroom. I put her in the closet, as she was fussing in distress.

Back in the living room, Sharon cried out for me to help her. Dad, pinning her down and unable to think clearly, shouted back, "Just go back to the room, Mandy!"

I couldn't. I didn't listen to him. Instead, I picked up our land-line and dialed 9-1-1. To this day I still don't know how the dispatchers were able to locate our house because I am certain I didn't have that address memorized, but they came at last.

The police. The ambulance. Child Protective Services.

When I close my eyes, I can still see the domestic dispute turned WWIII. I can still see Dad being handcuffed and shoved into the back of the cop car with its flashing lights, mouthing, "I'm sorry, kiddo" to me through the window. I can still see Sharon being strapped onto a stretcher and taken away in an ambulance. I can still remember longing for my mom.

I was shaken up. I felt so unsafe. I was desperate for control in the midst of complete chaos.

Little did I know that catastrophe in my childhood would become the catalyst for my calling. It woke me up to the reality that many boys and girls in this world are in need of a temporary safe place. I wouldn't have known that unless I'd been one of them myself. It was also the very incident that made me understand how a child could long for their birth parents even after all they did wrong. Because I too still love my dad even after everything he's done.

God used that terrible day to plant the seeds in my heart for foster care and adoption. There's never been a clearer or greater desire in my life.

I could have grown up, pretended none of it happened, and kept it a secret. I could have believed it was my fault, or blamed God for allowing it to happen. I could have gone on to repeat the trauma and sins of my parents, but living consciously is about doing the inner work so that I don't.

While we don't have control over everything, especially our childhoods, living consciously is taking control of what we can. It's about thinking through our decisions and living intentionally rather than reactively or mindlessly. It's about living lives we're proud of rather than settling for the ones that befall us.

Am I Living Unconsciously?

If you're drifting through life, feel out of control, or don't know how you got here, you might be living unconsciously.

Do you find yourself wasting your time doing things that aren't important rather than focusing on completing what is important? Are you constantly caught up in drama? Did you go after the job you're in, or did you stumble into it by default? Are you spending your time doing busywork rather than what you want to do? Do you find yourself living from paycheck to paycheck or in debt, not knowing where your money goes?

There are so many questions I could ask and things we can consider, but I bet you already know if (or in which areas) you're living unconsciously. Because you are so smart, I'll put it this way: Do you feel like life is happening to you rather than *through* you? Are you on autopilot? Who has control of the steering wheel that is your life?

How to Live More Consciously

Living consciously isn't a one-and-done thing. It's a lifestyle, an art, a practice. It's a habit we can intentionally develop throughout the course of our lives.

It's so deceptively simple, yet the majority of people don't do it. Instead, we do what we've always done because it's what we're used to doing. It's easier that way, especially if we want to avoid processing hard truths.

The answer to living more consciously is to bring whatever is bubbling up from our subconscious into our conscious minds. In simpler terms, to think about everything deeply.

Personally, I live consciously by reflecting daily. I assess my mission and get clear on what it is I'm trying to do with my life. I review my relationships and think honestly about how I'm serving others and the impact they have on me. I consider my impact on the world and how my decisions affect other people, the environment, and my community at large. I consider the costs of my purchases and commitments. I audit my time and face the reality of too many hours spent on social media more frequently than I'd like to admit. I explore what kind of person I am becoming, what my values are, and whether or not I'm proud of what I find.

In order to reflect, you have to have space in your life. In order to act upon your reflections, you have to live at a slower pace. You cannot change what you think, say, or do when you're living at 90 mph. Our pace is a true matter of the heart. I am super passionate about space because it's the work that ultimately led me here. In my thirty-day devotional, *Space*, I talk about how vital space is for my ongoing transformation.

Think about it for yourself. When you have a jam-packed schedule, do your friends and family get your best? While you might be able to pull off a pleasant sixty-second interaction at the grocery store, what about the people closest to you? Are they recipients of your love, kindness, patience, and gentleness?

When we operate at or near our full capacity, we don't have time for interruptions. We miss out on opportunities. Yet I would argue this is where God is primarily found: in the space and interruptions of daily life.

It is in the space of our lives where we come face-to-face with ourselves and the not-so-pretty parts of life. We notice things we don't necessarily want to deal with, things that would be much easier to avoid by staying busy and not having any margin. Things like recognizing an unmet expectation in your marriage, feeling uncomfortable when you aren't producing, or fearing you've missed out on an awesome opportunity (or even worse, that you weren't invited).

But God calls us to a life so much richer than one spent busying ourselves to avoid hard things. He is there for us, and his Word reminds us that we don't have to be afraid. We can face whatever bubbles up to the surface in the spaces of our lives. It won't be painless, but it will be less painful than avoiding the truth and hiding behind our ridiculously overwhelming schedules.

Let's break down how living consciously and intentionally looks in daily life. As a foster parent, me living consciously looks like being cautious with what I share publicly and partnering with my children's parents rather than sharing for praise and compliments. It means that when a mom is late for a visit because she's busy getting her tongue pierced, I won't scold her in front of the kids. Rather, I'll wait to have a discussion with her about priorities once I've cooled down and when we can be alone, because I know how my words could impact the kids' view of her. It means that when I want to vent by posting (which is public) about something one of our kids did, I consider how they would feel if they read it at some point. It means I am constantly having to check myself, but the work is worth it because relationships are at stake.

As a wife, me living consciously looks like action instead of excuses. Rather than wishing I'd be more present when I'm at home with Eric or making excuses about how I use my phone for work, I find a way to take action in the direction I know I want to head. One way this has played out is by keeping my phone at a charging station in our kitchen, not in our bedroom.

With work, me living consciously means having boundaries about hours I'm "off" and not answering emails, clear communication, and structure. Innovation is a benefit of living consciously. No one creates anything new when they live unconsciously, on autopilot.

Within friendships, me living consciously means listening to hear rather than to respond. It means showing up instead of just saying "I'll pray about it." It requires being thoughtful about how my friends receive love and what they need in their current phase of life, especially if it's not the same as me. It means loving them so well it costs me at times.

Even with my space, living consciously is a choice I must make. Will I use my space to check in or numb out? Will I create space in my life and then use it to scroll mindlessly and binge-watch Netflix for hours on end, or will I spend a good portion of my space looking inward, evaluating, and caring for my soul?

Motives Matter

I attended a John Mayer concert in Indianapolis what feels like a decade ago and was enthralled by his skills even though I know absolutely nothing about guitar. John Mayer captivates his audience not only because he's so good at what he does but because he makes it look effortless. It seemed to me like he forgot he was playing in front of thousands, and his performance felt like a peek into his heart.

Whether you're driven by undeniable passion or the pressure to prove, it shows. This is why our motives matter. Motive is the primary work of a life lived consciously. In everything we think, say, and do, we must pause to consider, *Why? Am I trying to make myself look better? Is this for money, fame, or status? Am I seeking value or approval through this? Is my ego in check?*

Don't Live Up to Your Full Potential

We mustn't confuse living consciously with living out our full potential, which is a popular phrase I constantly see all over Pinterest, and it's in every self-help book I've ever read. "You can do it! Live up to your full potential!" they say. While I understand the sentiment, I think it leads us down a dark and dangerous path. It drives us to hustle and prove our worth—worth that we already know hinges not on what we can do but on a God who loves us unconditionally.

For those of us who follow Jesus, this is especially important. Why? Because Jesus didn't live up to his full potential.

Think about it. By our earthly standards and human measurements, Jesus, the Son of God, did not accomplish nearly as much as he could have! I mean, Jesus had all the power in the world. He could've stopped the Romans from crucifying him. He could've struck them all dead if he wanted. He healed people through his words and touch, so we know he had that kind of power. Yet there were so many situations where Jesus didn't exercise it. Jesus was God in the flesh, yet he rested and took naps. Living up to his full potential could have meant no resting, with so much work to be done. He had people to heal and parables to tell, yet he didn't set strict boundaries with his time like someone would do if trying to live up to their full potential. Jesus wouldn't have settled for only twelve disciples, either. Instead, he would've networked with a greater number of people to accomplish more and go further faster.

But that was not the way of Jesus. When I look at Jesus's ministry life here on earth, it's clear that he didn't live up to his full potential by our standards; rather, he fulfilled his commitments one at a time, and he accomplished the mission God gave him.

We can choose to follow Jesus haphazardly or we can take it seriously and be intentional. Living consciously as a Christ-follower means we fulfill our commitments one at a time. We can live out our purpose rather than striving to live up to some perceived notion of our potential.

The Difference between Desire and Calling

To live out our purpose on purpose, we have to discern between our own desires and our true callings. Now, here's the truth: I believe God gave you desires for a reason. There's no rule book that defines a calling. However, if you're seeking help discerning whether something is a mission God has put before you or a desire you have that might actually be a "good distraction," here are three litmus tests, so to speak.

Persistent Nudge

First, if there's one thing I know to be true of a calling, it's that it will stand the test of time. It will never just fade away. I don't know about you, but I change my mind a lot. One day I want my hair to be blonde, the next day I want it to be brown. One day I want to live in Chicago, the next day I dream of living in warmer

124

weather. You get the point. One thing that I've never been wishy-washy about, however, is the desire to care for children whose families are in crisis. I have never not wanted to do it; it's a part of me that's never faded. In fact, it was a nonnegotiable when I met my now-husband. Even years later, having experienced some of the hard, broken, and messy parts of the child welfare system, I would never want to give it up. The nudge to continue bringing in children and caring for them until they can reunite with their mommy or daddy has never been absent from my life.

Premised on Love

Second, I don't believe that a true calling from God will ever come from a place of revenge or hate, a desire to get rich, or a longing for attention. It is rooted in love. Your calling will stem from a desire to serve love in a broken, messy world. It might not look like Mother Teresa's calling, and that's OK. Maybe you've always struggled with gender equality, and you feel called to start a software company where all women are paid equal to men. Maybe you struggled with reading as a child, and you're called to be a reading specialist or a speech pathologist for kids just like you.

I can't guarantee that your calling will lead to a big salary, but I do believe it will lead to a purposeful life. And a purposeful life is a happy one. You might be on a stage or at a desk, you might be making six figures or just enough to cover your expenses, but I know that it matters and that—if it's truly your calling—you'll do it from a place of love.

Leap of Faith and Sacrifice

Three, if something is not your calling, it will be easy. It will look like everyone else's choices, probably. It will be safe. If your nudge is pushing you to do something that scares you or isn't what all your friends are doing, pay attention. It might be your calling. If your nudge requires a sacrifice of you, maybe even a really big one, lean in.

125

I don't know if your leap of faith will be to drop out of college and fly across the world to serve in a different country for a year or if it will look like changing majors or starting an Etsy shop. I don't know if it will happen in one giant leap or a million baby leaps like mine. I've known that I'm called to be a foster mom for years now. But more recently I'm listening to the nudge on my heart to share truth and speak to the hard things we'd all rather avoid and pretend don't exist, things like sin and shame. This calling has led me to quit my job and to begin to fully reveal who I am without needing to know I will receive acceptance. And none of these things have happened overnight. Most callings don't.

We have to remember that God calls us to a life of faith. Our faith leads us to our dreams and calling. We don't have to go searching for them. If God called us to live safe, manageable lives, then we wouldn't really need him. Our sweet spot is when we are positioned to rely fully on him.

What God wants to do through you is beyond you. He wants to put you on display to the world, showing what he is able to do through a life of faith. We can't live out our calling without him—if we can, it's not our calling!

What is the dream in your heart?

Where do you feel a discontent you can't ignore?

What's the junk you've lived through that you're meant to help others get through now too?

After college, I was a high school Spanish teacher. Then an elementary school teacher. Then I randomly switched to a job in marketing as the global media manager for a huge company. After that, I worked at my church. For now, I write, speak, and parent children through foster care.

Your calling is not the same as your career. Sometimes these two things converge, sometimes they do not. Either way, it usually takes a bunch of tries and failures to get clear on what you were truly made for. Don't shy away from change or from trying something you might fail. Listen to God's gentle nudge. Risk it all by relying on him. That's how you end up living out your calling.

So here's what I want you to do, God helping you: Take your everyday, ordinary life—your sleeping, eating, going-to-work, and walking-around life—and place it before God as an offering. Embracing what God does for you is the best thing you can do for him. Don't become so well-adjusted to your culture that you fit into it without even thinking. Instead, fix your attention on God. You'll be changed from the inside out. Readily recognize what he wants from you, and quickly respond to it. Unlike the culture around you, always dragging you down to its level of immaturity, God brings the best out of you, develops well-formed maturity in you. (Rom. 12:1–2 Message)

SOUL CARE PRACTICE NO. 8
Exercise mindfulness.

Be Radically Honest with Yourself

1. Which catastrophes in your life might be the catalyst of your calling?
2. In which areas of your life are you living on autopilot instead of consciously?
3. When is the last time you put your phone down, took a deep breath, and observed how you felt inside?
4. Rate the pace of your life. Do you need to slow down and create margin?
5. What would it look like for you to live out your purpose?

CHAPTER 9

All the Things We Cannot See

A couple of years ago, my husband and I made the two-hour drive back to our Indiana roots to attend our nephew's birthday party.

We planned on seeing my mom one of the evenings during our stay, but the details were loose in my mind. I thought we would arrive at Mom's house around 6:00 p.m. and maybe go out for dinner or something.

Lo and behold, the details weren't loose in my mom's mind. Without ever clearly communicating it to us, she planned for our prompt arrival at 6:00 and made a dinner reservation for 6:30. She was excited and couldn't wait for a fun evening with us!

You can imagine my confusion when we arrived at her house around 6:30 and found Mom in a sour mood. After arguing for a few minutes, we hashed out the details, and it all began to make sense. She was disappointed. She felt like I didn't care about her or respect our time together. She had expectations of what our time together was going to look like, and when reality did not align, she was both sad and frustrated.

Once we talked everything through, we both recognized the errors in our communication. I apologized and reminded her that if I had known she was counting on us arriving at a very specific time and had made a dinner reservation, we would've absolutely been prompt. But I couldn't meet an expectation I didn't know existed. She acknowledged that she knew I would never intentionally ruin our plans together, and we worked through it. Today we're able to laugh about it.

My mom isn't the only one guilty of not clearly communicating expectations. In friendships and in my marriage, I've created expectations but never shared them clearly, and then felt disappointed by the people I love—who never even knew they let me down.

We can't expect people to meet our needs or show up for us in the way we desire if we don't voice those things. In addition to recognizing the need to clearly communicate expectations, one of the other biggest takeaways from that day with Mom was the importance of giving each other the benefit of the doubt. It's the healthiest way to approach every difficult situation or conversation—but I'm not saying it'll be easy.

Believe me when I say that people are not out to get you! Nine times out of ten, they aren't trying to upset you. Whether it's because they said something or didn't say anything, did something or didn't do anything, choose to give them the benefit of the doubt. Be quick to forgive. If it still bothers you a few days later, you can always revisit the issue.

One way I've grown in this area is by asking myself, *Are they intentionally [fill in the blank] to hurt me?* They probably have no idea how they are making you feel. Then, when the time is right, speak up about it to clear the air so that the situation doesn't fester or repeat.

Expectations Are Powerful

I was raised to be suspicious about people and their motives, to not trust until trust had thoroughly been earned. I honestly didn't know there was any other way to live, until I met Eric. He believed in giving people the benefit of the doubt: when you have the possibility of believing something good or something bad about someone, choose to believe the good.

We were newly dating when he drove us out to his friend's house in the country for a bonfire. In the car, I began to feel anxious. I told him that I just knew it was going to be a horrible time for me. The other women there were going to be cliquey, I was going to be left out of the conversation, and no one was going to make any effort to get to know me.

When we arrived, my prophecy was fulfilled. The other women huddled around a firepit together, I wasn't really included in the conversation, and I noted all of the ways I wasn't like any of them in my mind. It was as horrible of a time for me as I'd expected it would be.

Much to my surprise, a few days later I received an invitation to another one of these hangouts, but this time it was just for the women. I wasn't sure why I got invited, but Eric encouraged me to go. He told me to give them the benefit of the doubt this time, so I decided to try my best in doing so. Guess what happened? It was such a fun evening with those same women whom I'd previously felt terrible around. The only thing that had shifted was my mindset.

I realized then that we will always find what we look for. Expectations have a very curious aspect: the negative ones seem to always be met. So, if you expect another person to be nasty and spiteful to you, you'll perceive that they are nasty and spiteful to you. If you expect to be lonely and sad, you know what? You will probably be lonely and sad. You will suffer because you expect to suffer.

We need to stop doing this! Don't expect the worst. Be more courageous than that. Expect positive interactions wherever you go. Show up ready to make those expectations a reality. If you anticipate having meaningful conversations, you probably will have meaningful conversations. You will have a good time because you expect to have a good time.

Thanks to my husband, I've learned that it's in our favor to give people the benefit of the doubt and only be disappointed every now and then, rather than be cynical about everyone and be hurt 100 percent of the time. After all, it's hard to connect with anyone if you're always skeptical of them.

Cures for Common Comparison

If only resisting the urge to think the worst about others was where our inner work came to an end! We also have to stop comparing ourselves to others. I love what Bob Goff says about comparison: "We won't be distracted by comparison if we're captivated with purpose."[1] It's so true. When we live conscious lives with greater intentionality, we shouldn't have much energy left for comparison. However, it's always going to be a thing that creeps in if we aren't cautious, so here are three of my favorite antidotes for comparison.

Create

First, create. I don't know who said, "You'll never be criticized by someone doing more than you," but they were onto something. Think about it. People who are doing big and faithful things with their lives, such as starting nonprofits, running businesses, raising children, and more don't have time to criticize or compare themselves or their work to others. If you're drowning in comparison, consider creating something. You may not believe it, but you are an artist. Just look at the sunset, the ocean, or your closest friends for proof of God's artistry. And you are created in his image. God passed his creativity down to you. When you use it, you glorify him.

I often hear, "I'd love to do that, but I'm not creative." In fact, I used to say that myself. I was so scared of what others might think that I kept all of my ideas and unique forms of expression to myself for many years. But the capacity to create exists within each of us. You might be a medical student, math teacher, lawyer, or accountant. You might call yourself "anything but creative," but I'm willing to bet you're wrong. Creativity is in your DNA. It can look like a whole bunch of different things—painting, cooking, photography, organizing, sewing, decorating, putting together outfits, reading, writing, playing music, collecting things, and the list goes on. Think about what you can create to add value to your community. Get lost in it.

Concentrate

Second, concentrate. If you find yourself constantly comparing yourself or aspects of your life to other people, you can't possibly be living consciously. Shift your focus inward. You might be thinking, *But Manda, isn't it selfish to think about myself more than other people?* Don't worry; we'll get to that more specifically later in this chapter. For now, consider the amount of time you spend observing and thinking about the people around you.

Instead of focusing on Lisa's beautiful form in barre class, shift your focus back to your own form. After all, she doesn't realize you think she's amazing— unless you tell her, of course, which is actually another great way to channel your comparison for good—so you might as well focus on improving your own technique and perhaps prevent an injury.

One time I was in line at Panera, excited to order my favorite: broccoli cheddar soup. The woman in front of me was beautiful and thin. I was at my heaviest weight, but even more problematic than a few extra pounds were my struggles with depression and acne. As I concentrated on the beautiful girl in front of me, I only felt worse about myself. *How does she maintain such a beautiful figure? What skincare products does she use? Is that her natural hair, or are those extensions?* I thought about ordering a salad instead. Then I made a conscious effort to concentrate on myself: *Manda, be proud of yourself! You got out of bed to meet a friend here when you've felt like disappearing altogether. You love broccoli cheddar soup, and this will be a moment of joy for your tastebuds today. Your body needs something other than candy right now. Baby steps in the right direction. You are doing great.*

Concentrating on ourselves requires talking back to our inner critic. We can't expect to always be in a season of ease or goodness. When we're in the midst of hard things like depression, divorce, or transitioning new kids in or out of our lives, just to name a few examples, we need to be concentrating on ourselves rather than wasting energy (which is especially precious in hard times) on other people.

When an acquaintance of mine got a book deal long before I did, I was instantly filled with envy as I compared my work to hers. *My writing is objectively better than hers! How in the world did she get that deal? Her audience isn't nearly as engaged as mine. Who is taking her photos? I wonder how she made a sign-up form like that.* I dug into her website and social media, spending hours (not my finest day) picking apart how I would do it all differently (ahem, better) than her. I threw a pity party for myself too. Finally, when that got old, I made the choice to put up my blinders and concentrate on my own work. After creating something I was really proud of, I realized how much sooner I could've done so had I not been so consumed by watching and comparing myself to other writers.

Celebrate

Last, but certainly not least, celebrate. Celebrate yourself and celebrate other people. See if you can be the loudest cheerleader for everyone around you, no matter what's going on in your life. The more you celebrate, the less likely you'll be having a pity party for one. It might feel insincere at first, but you can celebrate your way out of comparison if you really want to.

When someone you know books a trip to Bali, and you haven't had a vacation in years, it's easy to feel a twinge of jealousy and compare your financial state or intricate life details to theirs. When someone you know gets pregnant on the first try and you have been trying for fourteen months, how could you not compare your body, sex life, and overall health to theirs? It could be anything—a home renovation, a job promotion, an engagement. Comparison whispers, "You're falling behind," or "They have it all," or "When will it be my turn?" But celebration says, "If it can happen for her, it can happen for me too," and "I'm going to be joyful for them because they will be joyful for me when my time comes," and "Even though I don't have what I want, I am so glad one more person does."

Celebrating requires us to believe in abundance; there is more than enough for all of us. Remember, there aren't limited quantities of babies, marriages, and promotions. The universe isn't keeping score, so don't allow your mind to go there. Someone else's dream coming true does not decrease your chances.

Social Media

My friend Jason Miller is the founding pastor of South Bend City Church. Eric lived with Jason throughout our entire dating relationship, and the two of them have well over a decade of friendship under their belt, so naturally he's become more like a big brother to me. Since South Bend is our hometown and Jason is one of the best, most thoughtful communicators of our generation, we always attend whenever we're there for a weekend.

I've never forgotten one of his sermons because it was unlike anything I'd ever heard before. He shared findings from a research study that had been conducted to see how social media impacted mental health. I thought for sure he was going to say that social media was bad for us, and that Jesus wouldn't have had it if he were living among us today. Even though I use it, I assumed he was going to tell us all about the negative impact our apps have on our mental health, but what he ended up sharing surprised me.

Researchers found that people who were on social media as observers—those who did not really participate by posting, liking, or commenting—had negative thoughts about themselves and the world at large at the end of their time spent. On the other hand, people who actively engaged—those who did post, like, and comment—during the same allotted time on those same apps were significantly happier. It wasn't the amount of time or the specific social media channels that made a difference but rather how the user engaged. Two people could use Instagram for exactly the same amount of time yet have vastly different outcomes based on whether they participated or simply observed.

For me to stay healthy and care for my soul, online limitations and sometimes monthlong breaks are necessary. You'll have to decide for yourself what health on social media looks like. You can abandon it altogether or retrain yourself to use it healthily. Here are my top suggestions, based on Jason's sermon and on current research.

1. *Be active, not passive.* Instead of just scrolling, actively engage with other people's content. Practice celebrating.
2. *Set time limits.* If it's taking away time with your kids, spouse, or friends, you'll want to realign your priorities. If it's robbing you of sleep, get disciplined with boundaries for yourself. There's even a time limit feature you can set for yourself on Instagram. I have been using it for months now, and it's been really helpful.
3. *Be intentional.* Question your motives behind what you choose to share and how you interact. Use social media from a place of wholeness, not as a place to get your fix or affirmation.

More than anything else, I've found it helpful to avoid getting on the internet when I'm bored, as that never produces any good fruit and only leads to mindless scrolling and wasted time. Use your favorite apps as a way to stay connected with and cheer on the people who matter most in your life.

Focusing Inward without Becoming Self-Absorbed

Carl Jung, a psychiatrist whose work has been deeply meaningful in my life, said, "Until you make the unconscious conscious, it will direct your life and you will call it fate."[2] I could have chosen not to look inward and never discover the real reasons behind all that I think, say, believe, or do. I would have continued making choices that ultimately hurt myself, my friends, my marriage, and my work. I probably would also have made excuses, tried to justify myself, and promised up and down that I'd never do it again.

However, without getting to the root and bringing my darkness into the light (or in other words, from my unconscious to conscious mind), I would have been trapped in a cycle of repeating bad habits and making mistakes. I probably would've called it fate and blamed it on bad luck or other external factors. Heck, I might have even come to a point where I chalked my sin up as being part of my identity. *I'm a cheater. I'll never change. I'm a gossiper. That's just my personality.*

That's what the Enemy wants us to do, because if we believe we're no good and are unable to overcome sin, then we can't be beacons of love and hope in the world. Bringing everything that's dark and unconscious within us to the light, where it is conscious and known, is the hardest, bravest, and most transformative work we can do for ourselves and those we love.

There is a distinct difference between doing this inner work and being self-absorbed. I often have people say to me, "But Manda, doing all of this work that focuses on myself feels selfish!" I remind them, time and time again, that doing the work is necessary. It's *not* doing the work that's selfish. I'll go as far as saying that by looking inward we can love others better.

If I had just carried on living trapped in my sin and darkness, not focusing on myself because "it's too selfish," then I would have continued to hurt my husband, our marriage, and myself. If a mom doesn't eat well or make time for exercise to take care of her body because "it's too selfish," then she will very likely have less time with her kids in the long run because her health will decline at an earlier age.

It's not "too selfish" to decline a party invite when you're working on your sobriety. It's not "too selfish" to pay for therapy when you have trauma to work through. It's not "too selfish" because our souls are at stake! If we choose not to look inward and deal with the unhealthiness we notice within ourselves, we're not only hurting ourselves but other people as well.

I first started going to counseling because I wanted and desperately needed help recovering from childhood wounds and trauma. I stayed in therapy long after I made progress in those things because I noticed how much of my inner work had a direct correlation with other people. The focus is on myself, but my reason for showing up and going is truly about those I love. I do my inner work because:

I love my kids. I don't want to be a mother who constantly micromanages her children.

I love my husband. I don't want a just OK marriage when it can be thriving.

I love my friends. I don't want to push people away because I'm unaware of how I come across.

I used to think I went to counseling because I hated myself. Now I realize it's quite the opposite.

When you own a car, you have to take care of it, right? You have to get the oil changed, rotate the tires (I'm really bad at remembering this one!), and change the filters, along with topping off the other fluids and replacing the brakes when they get worn. If you didn't do those things, then your car wouldn't function optimally. It would end up having significant issues that cost a lot more to repair than if you'd kept up with ongoing maintenance in the first place. The same goes for taking care of yourself—and I'm talking specifically about your soul right now, because I think there's enough information out there constantly reminding us to take care of our bodies.

You can't just put gas in the tank and go through the car wash every so often and expect your car to last you for years. You have to keep up with routine maintenance that is unseen but vital. Similarly, you need to regularly do maintenance on the inner workings of you.

Think about it like this: When you feel at home in yourself—when you are happy, healthy, and balanced—are you more likely to give? More likely to forgive? More available to others? I know for me the answer is obvious. And that is precisely why inner work is one of the least selfish practices on the planet. It directly impacts everyone around us.

If I give everything I own to the poor and even go to the stake to be burned as a martyr, but I don't love, I've gotten nowhere. So, no matter what I say, what I believe, and what I do, I'm bankrupt without love.

> Love never gives up.
> Love cares more for others than for self.
> Love doesn't want what it doesn't have.
> Love doesn't strut,
> Doesn't have a swelled head,
> Doesn't force itself on others,
> Isn't always "me first,"
> Doesn't fly off the handle,
> Doesn't keep score of the sins of others,
> Doesn't revel when others grovel,
> Takes pleasure in the flowering of truth,
> Puts up with anything,
> Trusts God always,
> Always looks for the best,
> Never looks back,
> But keeps going to the end. (1 Cor. 13:3–7 Message)

SOUL CARE PRACTICE NO. 9

Invest in your unseen self.

Be Radically Honest with Yourself

1. When have you been given the benefit of the doubt, and have you offered the same in return?

2. Are you prone to setting positive or negative expectations, and how does that impact your daily life?

3. What rises up within you when you see someone else thriving?

4. Why do you stay on social media, and how does it impact the inner, unseen parts of yourself?

5. Do you believe it's selfish to invest in your health? Why or why not?

CHAPTER 10

It's Not Them, It's You

When we first became foster parents, I was naïve about many of the complexities surrounding the children in our care and their biological families. While my intentions weren't bad, looking back, I can see I made a lot of stupid comments. Being that Eric and I were the first of our friends and our close-knit community in Chicago to foster, no one really noticed or chose to say anything about how I was coming across. Until one day a church acquaintance interrupted me midsentence to correct something I had just stated. She pointed out that the way I was speaking about one of our children's biological parents wasn't OK. She was firm, and I felt attacked. Initially, I tried to swallow my pride as I blinked back tears. I felt caught off guard and exposed. I then tried to clarify what I meant and defend myself. She wasn't interested. She went on to tell me that it seemed like I had the air of a white savior complex about me. She said a few other things too, but my ears had stopped working. I thought my jaw was going to hit the floor.

Me, a white savior? For those of you who aren't familiar, the white savior complex is when white people "help" nonwhite people in a way that is harmful and is based in the belief that people of color are unable to solve their own problems. It implies that they need saving, and that white people are the only ones competent enough to do so.

It felt horrible to be accused of such a thing, and I became very angry. I abruptly ended our discussion by using my husband as an excuse to get out of this awkward ambush.

The entire train ride home, I vented to Eric about how rude this woman was for saying what she said. He nodded along, mostly comforting me and giving me the liberty to speak my mind. Throughout that entire afternoon and evening, her words permeated my mind. Naturally, I began one hundred rebuttals.

I'm not a white savior! I didn't choose to care for black and brown children; they just happened to be the ones we received a call for. I didn't choose to be white. I'm not trying to save anybody. I'm just trying to help care for these precious children!

I spiraled quickly.

Who is she to judge me? Is she stepping up to care for kids in need? NO! Then she can mind her own business. Whatever happened to the rule, "If you don't have anything nice to say, don't say anything at all"? Why does race have to get brought into this, anyhow?

Within a few weeks, I couldn't take it anymore. I kept ruminating on her accusation. I grew increasingly hostile each time I saw her. But as time went on, I began to feel a deep conviction weighing on my conscience. I spent time in silence with myself and with God. I prayed about it, which led me to realize I should defend myself less and instead look inward to see if any of her words might be true.

I met with my incredible mentor turned friend, Rocio, and told her about the conversation and how that statement was weighing me down. She said, "Manda, that's because when people say things about us like that, we don't need to ask *if* it's true but rather *how* it's true."

Gulp. I didn't want to consider that what the woman said might have some truth to it. I didn't want to face the dark parts of my altruism. Yet I dug deeper, and I realized there was some real truth to her accusation.

Rocio also reminded me that this was why it's so important to ask people if we can give them feedback before we do it. She pointed out how I didn't have much relational equity with that woman, which is why I was extra defensive.

I discovered a lot from a woman who looked me in the eyes and told me a painful truth about myself. I learned I needed to take ownership of my failures. I learned that feedback and truth-telling should be between people who have relational equity. Even still, we owe each other the decency to ask permission before spilling the tea. Most importantly, I ended up learning how to stop being a white savior.

Information is literally at our fingertips, so let's not make excuses to justify our behaviors. For me, a simple google search, "How to stop being a white savior," led me to the following answers:

1. *Promote dignity.* Respect all different types of people. Remember that while you might have your differences, you aren't better than anyone else.

2. *Gain informed consent.* Respect people's privacy and ask permission before sharing images or stories about them. Ask yourself, "How will they feel if/when they see it?"

3. *Question your intentions.* This is another reminder about conscious living. What's the "why" behind your sharing and doing? Is it about you or being perceived as a "good person" more than it is about the actual work and people you're caring for?

4. *Dismantle stereotypes.* Find ways to share and tell people information that widens their perspective and challenges

their way of thinking about whole groups of people. Look for the ways you're alike instead of focusing on the ways you're different.[1]

Have I gotten it right as a foster parent all of the time since that interaction four years ago? No. Have I perfectly followed Jesus and helped those who are vulnerable and oppressed ever since? No. Will there always be people lurking around online just waiting for opportunities to call others out? Yes.

But none of this means we should stop paying attention, seeking greater self-awareness, and pursuing a conscious life with pure motives.

Our Shadow Side

I know I'm not supposed to admit this as a self-proclaiming follower of Jesus, but there are just some people I have a really hard time liking.

Years ago when I taught at our local elementary school, I had a colleague who was around the same age as me who drove me absolutely nuts. She always went above and beyond both inside and outside the classroom, she was a total suck-up to our principal, and she never failed to go around to the other teachers in her pod to ask how she could best support them that week. Objectively, she was a really kind person, so why did I feel so annoyed every time I was around her? Furthermore, why didn't anyone else seem even mildly irritated by her?

Was my reaction driven by her self-righteous attitude? The fact that she was kind of a know-it-all? Always seeking attention?

Just like there are parts of our bodies and appearance we don't like when we look in the mirror, there are also aspects of our personalities we don't want to accept. The things we hate the most in other people are actually inside us, at least in a symbolic way.

To put it another way: what we dislike in others is also what we dislike about ourselves.

We are constantly projecting parts of ourselves. Since we're not usually able to see our own shadows, life gives us the gift of relationships. Relationships show us what we have inside. People act like mirrors, reflecting and giving us a chance to see who we are.

Perhaps I felt annoyed by my colleague because the things I perceived about her were true. Or maybe she was reflecting the very things I didn't like about myself on a deep level. This concept is often referred to as our shadow side.

Our shadows contain parts of ourselves we don't like and have probably disowned or subconsciously denied having. They are the things we try to hide and suppress. When these unfavorable qualities, habits, or tendencies reveal themselves through other people, we get so bothered, but our reaction is really about our own shortcomings. The things about other people that bother us, irritate us, get under our skin, and drive us crazy are more often than not our own unacknowledged or rejected issues.

This is why it's important to ask ourselves the question, *What's going on in my heart?*

I came to realize that my fellow teacher was triggering me because I could see in her the parts of myself I didn't like—my desire for approval and affirmation from others and my pride being at the top of the list. My heart was filled with judgment as I viewed her through a critical, narrow lens.

Jesus Is the Master Mirror Holder

In chapter 2, I shared how important it is to find a trusted mirror. You have mirrors around you at all times through other people, if you view them as such—but Jesus is the master mirror holder.

In Matthew 5–7, Jesus gives his longest moral teachings in the Sermon on the Mount, which have become central tenets of

Christian discipleship. Jesus addresses our judgment of others in Matthew 7:3–5 when he says,

> Why do you look at the speck of sawdust in your brother's eye and pay no attention to the plank in your own eye? How can you say to your brother, "Let me take the speck out of your eye," when all the time there is a plank in your own eye? You hypocrite, first take the plank out of your own eye, and then you will see clearly to remove the speck from your brother's eye.

Jesus reminds us that the minute we see things within other people that we don't like (whether a reflection about something within ourselves or not), we have no business calling them out or casting judgment, because we have our own issues to work through.

Nothing outside of You Has Power over You

Our three boys argued nonstop, so most days I felt like a taxi driver by day and a referee by night. Recently our oldest, Goof, had been instigating our middle child, Bear, as if looking for a fight. In the car one morning, Bear told me he woke up in the middle of the night from a bad dream and got himself a glass of water. Goof invited himself into the conversation with, "Bro, no you didn't. Why you lyin'?" Bear snapped back, and the two were at war, as usual. In my attempt to defuse their senseless argument, I reminded Goof that for one, he had no idea what kinds of dreams other people had in their sleep, and two, there was a good chance he was zonked out when Bear woke up in the middle of the night to get a glass of water. But because kids are kids and siblings are the worst, my two big boys carried on in their most annoying fight to date . . .

"Bro, you do too much. You lyin' jussa get attention."

"No I ain't."

"Yes you is."

"No I ain't."

"Yes you is."

"Shut up."

"No, you shut up."

"Make me."

I kid you not, this went on for four minutes in the back seat—before they started punching each other, and then I got them both to zip it and keep their hands to themselves by threatening to take away Goof's phone and Bear's favorite toy.

Then I reminded Bear how important it is to ignore anyone who's trying to instigate and rile him up. I told all three of them for what felt like the thousandth time: you can't control other people; you can only control your reaction to them.

At dinner that evening, we went around the table modeling the beautiful concept of ignoring someone who is trying to pick a fight with you. Eric got super into it, of course; the kids laughed as he pretended to instigate a fight with me as I ignored him relentlessly and kept on eating my pizza in peace. Our boys loved this little "game" we played, and I think they started to catch on to the bigger lesson. Before bed that evening, I looked into their eyes and reminded each of them that there is nothing outside of them that has power over them.

Maybe you need to hear it too: nothing outside of you has power over you. Not your friends or your annoying coworker. Not your circumstances or your surroundings. Not your life coach or your parents. Maybe you feel stressed out because you feel the weight of that responsibility right now. I can assure you that there's nothing better than waking up to the reality that you have access to all the power within you. You can live a life you're proud of, if you want. You can stop taking the bait of other people's drama. You can maintain your composure even when chaos breaks loose in your home or at the office. The only things that actually have power over you live inside you. If you needed another reason to care about what's going on deep inside your soul, this is it.

True Ownership Includes No "Buts"

If we're going to be people who channel the power within us, we have to be owners. Just like you can't have action without awareness, you can't have transformation without ownership.

What I've loved most about owning a home is that I can do just about anything I want to it. I can paint and even remodel if I want to. Because it's "mine," I can transform the space if my little heart decides to channel her inner Joanna Gaines one day. If I were still renting, I wouldn't be able to because there are rules, and because I don't have money to invest in property that's not my own. The same is true for my inner world. If I own all that lives within me, I can heal and grow. If I don't own it, I won't invest in it.

I see this in people all too often. Here's the way it goes: their life is a mess filled with drama and destruction but—make no mistake—they never had any part in causing it. Or so they say. They act as if people barged into their house and made a mess while they stood there powerlessly. Take my extended family member, Janet, for example.

Janet's life spiraled downhill quickly as she blamed and justified everything in her life rather than taking ownership and seeking professional help for healing. Janet's marriage imploded when it came out that she had been having an affair. While I have no judgment toward her, I was devastated to read a lengthy update she shared on Facebook in which she justified her infidelity. She blamed it on the lack of attention she received from her husband. She admitted that what she had been doing for the last year was wrong, but he wasn't affectionate enough, never listened to her needs, and they lived like roommates.

The problem is the *but*.

She accepted fault only with disclaimers attached. To me, it was clear that her faithfulness was contingent upon someone else's behavior. (Talk about unsexy wedding vows . . . "I vow to stay faithful to you as long as you show me the right amount of affection every day, adhere to all of my needs, and make sure we never feel like roommates.") We can make excuses and justify certain behaviors or we can grow, but we cannot do both at the same time. Unless we grasp that we have total ownership over our decisions and actions in this life, we will always find a way to play the victim.

I saw this *but* pattern in Janet's life continue long after her divorce. She blamed being tired and overweight on the long hours at her job. She blamed her decision not to go back to college on her children. She was a victim to her circumstances and part of the "rough life club." You know that club, don't you? The one that meets for happy hour or over a latte, where members come to swap stories of how awful life has been to them. This club specializes in one-upmanship as well. It's a membership based on moaning, groaning, and avoiding accountability or responsibility at all cost. Doesn't it sound miserable? Maybe your eyes are growing wide as you realize you're a part of, or a leader in, the rough life club. I pray you don't slam this book shut and write me off as a mean girl. Instead, I pray you keep reading and lean in to the uncomfortable topics. If we're willing to get comfortable with the uncomfortable, we'll surely experience change.

Are You Ready to Take Ownership?

The first step isn't action but rather belief. Belief in our own agency. Without it, we will continue to deem everything someone else's fault, which is strikingly disempowering. When we believe in our own agency, we acknowledge that we are in control of our life and that no one else has power over our thoughts and behavior. Only then are we empowered to take responsibility for our choices and their consequences.

Before I hit my personal rock bottom, I lived in oblivion and denial of my struggle. I couldn't take ownership because I wasn't aware or ready. Perhaps I didn't fully believe in my own agency.

The reality is that sometimes things have to get worse before they can get better in order for us to be ready.

Inner Willpower

One of our former foster youth, Deja, now an incredible and grown woman, used to come back to stay with us every Sunday through Wednesday because our home was super close to the community college she attended. For the sake of her convenience and because we all got too attached, there was simply no better option.

I absolutely loved having her in our home. She was respectful and always lent a helping hand with dinner or our boys' homework if needed. She kept her area tidy and never failed to express her gratitude. Simply put, she was easy to host and even easier to love. However, when we first agreed on this arrangement, I didn't think about my natural tendency to micromanage and how that would play into things. Her first week of staying with us, I made sure she had her school supplies and her alarm set, so you can imagine the panic I felt when, the next morning, her room was dark and quiet when she was supposed to be getting ready. I knocked on the door a few times. She said, "I'm up!" and I urged her to hurry so she wouldn't be late. Then I hollered goodbye as I loaded up our boys to get them off to school.

Later that evening at dinner, I asked her how class was, and she replied that she was just "really tired" and had decided to catch up on sleep and skip class. She assured me that it wouldn't happen again, but I told her I didn't need the assurance. You see, I wasn't paying for her college—I had nothing invested in her decision. I wanted what's best for her. I wanted to see her break the chains of generational poverty in her biological family. But I had to be honest with her: "I can't want this for you more than you want it for yourself, Deja."

With tears in my eyes, I reminded her that this was her one and only precious life. I told her that we all make choices, and the accumulation of those choices, in large part, become the life we make. I admitted that I wanted better for her than the universe had set her up for. We talked about how she was destined for a life of financial struggle in so many ways, but that attending college and getting a degree could be the key to unlock new doors for her. I reiterated to her that I knew how badly she wanted to obtain her degree but asked if she was willing to do what it took to make it a reality. I explained that if I could do it all for her, I would. Because that's a mother's love. But I couldn't. And an even deeper layer of motherly love is surrendering control to let your children soar without you—even if it means they crash every now and then.

No One Is Exempt

I don't put people on a pedestal anymore. There is truly no such thing as "shocking" news to me. Is it because I'm cynical or think people are all evil within? No. I just know every single person is human and therefore a sinner. Each and every one of us is capable of really dark things, especially if we aren't living a life in the light.

Sadly, this is what we're seeing when well-known leaders and public figures take a great fall. Whether they are dubious with their taxes, found guilty of sexual misconduct, or something entirely different, we're seeing how the shadow side of a person always catches up to them. There isn't a single person who doesn't need to care for their soul and look inward. If we think we're higher than that, we're only fooling ourselves. I am so thankful for God's protection over my life. I never want a platform that my character cannot sustain.

Taking ownership requires radical honesty with ourselves. It's a vital part of soul care and a necessary step in our path toward living healed, whole, and free.

When I was a child, I talked like a child, I thought like a child, I reasoned like a child. When I became a man, I put the ways of childhood behind me. (1 Cor. 13:11)

SOUL CARE PRACTICE NO. 10
Take ownership consistently.

Be Radically Honest with Yourself

1. When have you felt defensive about something said to you, and how was there truth in it?
2. What is your shadow side?
3. How have you avoided ownership by using *but* to justify something unhealthy in your life?
4. Who or what have you allowed to have power over you?
5. Is there anyone you have placed on a pedestal, where they don't belong?

CHAPTER 11

What Dreams Are Made Of

Last Friday, Eric and I went to a Dodgers baseball game thanks to free tickets we received from a friend. We kept our son, Shia, at home with a babysitter, so it was truly a relaxing date night for us. On Saturday we slept in, walked to our favorite local coffee shop, and then went for a hike in the afternoon. We ended the day watching comedy and playing Scrabble. On Sunday we spontaneously decided to skip church and head to the beach. We didn't spend much money and had no agenda.

I'm not telling you about our weekend because I think you care what my family and I did. I'm sharing about it because it was everything my dreams are made of—yet I rarely have such dreamy weekends because I have so many other commitments. I say yes and commit to plans to please someone else before considering if it's what I really want. Suddenly I realize that it's been twelve weekends in a row of showing up for obligations or social interactions I'm dreading instead of enjoying my life.

Weekends without plans and time constraints are what my dreams are made of because they bring joy to my soul. What about you? Have you taken time to consider what your dream life looks like? Not just on the weekends but all the time? None of us knows how long we'll be here, so we need to make the time count. Living consciously and intentionally to bring meaning and beauty to the world is one way. Chasing our dreams and cultivating a life rich in joy is another.

I have learned that I need to say no more often in order to say yes to what my soul needs most. Yes to my husband. Yes to our son. Yes to leaving our phones behind while we hike. Yes to supporting local businesses. Yes to laughter, slowness, and being fully present in the moment. But all these yeses don't happen without saying no to a lot.

Space

There's a summer I'll never forget because it contains a moment that changed my life. I was out running by myself in our Chicago neighborhood at the time. The Midwest summer air was thick with humidity (brutal for all of us runners), but the sunshine had to be taken advantage of. My September birthday was inching closer, so I had begun praying for God to reveal what he might want for me in the coming year, as I typically do each year.

Now, before you begin to imagine this moment being more holy than it was, let me confess: Cardi B was blaring through my headphones. I wasn't praying the way we often think prayer looks like: hands folded in silence, head bowed, and eyes closed. I had been praying the way I most often do, simply talking to God internally. With eyes open, legs moving, sweat pouring, and a rapper keeping me on pace.

I have never experienced God's audible voice, but in one swift moment I heard the Spirit of God say *space*, and it was undeniable. It stopped me in my tracks. Some could argue that my own conscience was speaking, but regardless of whether we agree where the word came from, one thing was clear: I was supposed to pursue space.

What that one word meant felt very clear. I ran home at an even faster pace and told Eric about the divine moment I'd just experienced. I began taking the pursuit of space seriously, the way a woman does when she believes God is truly encouraging something for her best interest. It didn't all happen overnight, but little by little I began to see change.

Slowly I was converted from being an overextended and stressed-out person to someone who had a full life yet didn't feel frantic or busy. I was composed, not from trying but rather as a natural consequence of living a life with space.

All of the years prior, I had listened to my mind, which told me, *Keep going. Push. Hustle. You've got this.* This led to sleepless nights, workaholism, and stress. My pastor at the time, Jeanne Stevens, once looked me in the eye and said, "Manda, your mind lies, but your body tells the truth. This is one of God's greatest gifts to us and is worth paying attention to."

Your body whispers before it screams, so pay attention to it.[1]

What is your body trying to tell you? Is your eye twitching? Do you have abnormal bowel movements? Are you constantly fatigued? Are there any signals telling you that you need to give it more sleep and rest, or perhaps exercise and movement?

Pay attention to your thoughts. Grab a journal and spend a moment freewriting. Does your mind often feel frantic and cluttered? What keeps coming up? Are your thoughts anxiety-ridden or peaceful?

The pursuit of space is rooted in the belief that we are human beings, not human doings. We can't, nor should we try, to be productive every minute of every day, seven days a week. How often do you have space for spontaneity in your day? Do you experience God's presence in your life, or is your life so full that there's no space for interruption?

I regularly hear from people who say they feel spiritually dead inside. They tell me they don't have time for God or for caring for themselves well, but when I press in, they admit to spending hours every single day sucked into social media and Netflix. If you were to take inventory of your days, would you be proud of how your time is spent?

If you created a pocket of space—even just five minutes—to start being with God every day, what might it look like?

Our outer world can also be a good indication of our inner world. Consider your physical space, both the body and home you live in. What does your body need? What about your living space?

What would help you cultivate a thriving environment? More plants? Less impromptu shopping purchases? More frequent cleaning?

What hobbies do you allow time for in your life that have nothing to do with serving, monetizing, or striving at all? Think about things you do purely for unadulterated enjoyment.

When was the last time you created freely without pressure, other people's expectations, or trying to make a profit? It could look like a number of things: writing a poem, tackling a DIY project, or learning a TikTok dance.

Despite what you may have grown up hearing, God is delighted in his children feeling joyful.

Rhythm

Rhythm moves you. You dance to it, find your groove, let go a little, and enjoy the moment and see where it takes you. Routine, on the other hand—not so much. You march to routine. It's a steady metronome keeping time. And if you sway, if you linger, if you move out of order, or fail to complete a step, then you fail. You're out of time. You're lagging. Rhythm allows change and flexibility for different seasons in life, which is why I love the approach of rhythm so much more than routine. Every single one of us has routines, and many of us have rhythms too.

List out your rhythms and your routines. What makes you light up? What makes you feel bogged down? Is there any reason to continue those that leave your soul feeling depleted?

Creating space in our lives isn't just for us. When we have space and use it well, it's a gift to everyone around us. How much more can you intentionally love your family, friends, neighbors, and complete strangers if you have space in your days? What might you do if only you had the time? Make a list of ideas and put them into a jar. Once a week, on a day that you choose, use your space to intentionally serve others. A few ideas:

Make two lasagnas while you're at it and give one to a friend or neighbor.

Call your grandma or some other family member just to check in.

Offer to watch your friends' kids so they can go on a date night.

Ask your spouse or friend to go for a walk with you, and spend that time asking good questions and building them up.

Boredom

I can't recall the last time I felt bored. Was it during our family road trip across the country with nothing to do for hours on end except look out the window and make up games to play with my stepsisters?

Was it the last time I sat in front of our family's solo (very bulky) computer, eager to chat with friends on Myspace but forced to sit through minutes of a sound us '90s kids will never forget: dial-up internet? Was it all of the times I've stood in line for something but didn't have a cell phone to text someone or check any notifications?

Boredom is not when you have nothing to do. Boredom is what happens when you are no longer being stimulated. Fortunately, boredom is a gift no child asks for but almost every child receives. Unfortunately, boredom is now an endangered species, soon to be extinct.

My childhood is full of incredible things I did when I was bored. Boredom made an indoor skating rink in our unfinished basement with my stepsisters. Boredom went outside to catch tadpoles and lightning bugs in mason jars. Boredom cuddled up with Mom and asked questions like, "Want to play Hungry Hungry Hippos with me?"

When I first questioned why I no longer feel bored, my initial thought was *I'm a grown woman with big responsibilities, like caring for small humans and paying bills.* But then I realized it wasn't *just* because of that. I don't have time to be bored. Every minute of my day is accounted for because I am constantly connected.

We no longer sit and twiddle our thumbs while we're in line or in a waiting room. Our thumbs are too busy typing away on screens. Many of us rarely go out for dinner, a movie, or a walk without taking a photo and sharing private moments with the public.

Don't get me wrong—it's not all bad. It's just that when we are so constantly connected, we miss out on the present.

How many times have we missed out on a moment with our spouse or children or a friend because we were caught up in being connected with someone else through a screen? How many times have we missed out on opportunities for serendipitous moments and life-changing conversations with strangers because we chose to look down, swipe, and scroll instead of being right where our feet are?

We are constantly pursuing distractions, and we don't even know we're doing it, because that's become our way of existing in the world. Many of us don't even know how to feel at peace in our own company, and that is devastating.

There are so many upsides to downtime. From creativity to surprising encounters, increased rest to revolutionary thoughts, boredom is a preliminary piece to having your best days yet.

Quiet

One of my favorite things to do is meet up with a friend at a local coffee shop. I'm the friend who rarely turns down an invitation for meaningful conversations over an iced mocha. I'll ditch my phone and ask questions and lose track of time while I'm with people. But it wasn't always this way.

A few years ago, I met up with a friend at a Starbucks (long before my days of intentionally choosing to support local and small businesses) and left realizing a huge deficit within myself. You see, from the moment we arrived, I immediately began offering up what was going on in my life. I spilled the good, the hard, the new, and the juicy. I spoke so fast, barely inhaling for oxygen while rambling incessantly about every detail to catch her up on my life. My sweet friend nodded her head between bites of blueberry scone and sips of coffee.

Then she excused herself to use the restroom. When she returned to our table, she didn't sit back down. She pushed in her chair and mentioned how quickly an hour passed and said she needed to head home. We hugged and parted ways. It felt abrupt. My gut felt that something was off.

I sat for a minute, then began to realize I felt guilty and selfish for not asking how she was. I mulled over whether to say something or not. Finally, I decided to shoot her a quick text message. In it, I apologized for taking up our entire time talking about my life. I expressed how much it meant to me that we were able to spend time together.

She was kind but also honest in her response: "I would love to have another coffee date, but I need you to know that I also have things in my life I want to share with you. You never stop talking long enough to listen."

Ouch. Her words kept floating around in my head. *You never stop talking long enough to listen.* That feeling in the pit of my stomach hadn't misled me. It was not pleasant to hear at the time, but oh, how grateful I am to have received a truth that eventually made me more of who God created me to be.

I hadn't been a terrible listener only with this one friend. As her words replayed in my mind and I prayed about that day, it became clear that this was how I showed up in my relationship with God as well. I would go about my life, pausing only to talk his ear off and then moving on. *Go, go, go. Do, do, do. Don't stop moving. Talk, talk, talk. Repeat.* Not a moment to spare for listening and receiving.

Since that interaction and that gift of hard truth, God has continued to gently remind me that he has things he wants to share with me. I just have to stop talking, moving, and multitasking long enough to listen. Sometimes he wants to whisper how much he loves me. Other times he nudges me toward confession or redirects me, and many times he wants to reflect with me. Regardless, it's always a gift.

Without moments of quiet, there is no listening or receiving. With quiet, however, we are able to hear things that are normally muted by all of the surrounding noise. We are able to accept words of affirmation and words of encouragement from those who love us and have our best interest at heart.

God even speaks to us through our intuition, but without silence and the ability to be comfortable in solitude, we miss out. Life is loud and convoluted. We can't hear the small voice inside that guides our next right move if we are too busy chatting over it.

It is in quiet moments that we meet parts of ourselves that have been there all along—but are only now ready to come out. If you want more dreamy days and don't know where to start, take it from me: stop talking long enough to listen.

Replenishment

We are constantly overextending ourselves. If we notice a pattern in our lives, such as constantly running behind, forgetting important things, or feeling embarrassed about how we act, these are indicators that we need to be replenished. Replenishment allows us to bring our full, best self to the world. I didn't realize how weary my soul was until I participated in a Life Plan in May 2020. (No better time to reassess your entire life than in the midst of a pandemic, when the world is shut down and everything feels hopeless, right? Not sure what I was thinking, but it worked out all right.) The process that my incredible Life Plan facilitator, Neil, took me through revealed I was not replenishing myself regularly nor in all the necessary areas that make us whole: physically, intellectually, emotionally, and spiritually.

Replenishment fuels your life and feeds your soul. Replenishment consists of thoughtful, purposeful activities that help you to be more productive, more creative, and more engaged with people and projects in all domains of your life.

What replenishes one person will deplete another, so there is no list of ways to replenish that I can give you. It looks different for each of us, but below are some of the things I have recognized are replenishing for me:

- High-intensity workouts: doing CorePower yoga sculpt, running, or boxing at least three times a week for forty-five minutes replenishes me physically.
- Reading fiction: reading for even twenty minutes a day replenishes me intellectually. (Notice the specificity of fiction, because reading nonfiction serves an entirely different purpose in my life and does not typically leave me feeling replenished.)
- Engaging in deep and meaningful conversations: having these at least once a week keeps me replenished emotionally.
- Solitude with God: engaging in prayer and worship music on a daily basis, during a weekly Sabbath practice,

and through an annual solitude retreat replenishes me spiritually.

These aren't selfish endeavors or an escape—they are essential ingredients and complements to caring for my soul so that I can show up better for the rest of the world. If I am physically depleted, intellectually bored, emotionally starved, and spiritually disoriented, everyone around me will eventually sense this. This is why replenishment is vital: it has a ripple effect far beyond our reach.

Creating sustainable rhythms takes time, and you can't expect it to happen overnight, but implementing the following steps can help you get started in shifting yours.

1. Get honest about what your rhythms are or all that is lacking by taking inventory hour by hour throughout your day for an entire week.

2. Spot all of the wasted space and time spent doing things you don't actually want to do.

3. Note all of the places in your schedule you found enjoyment.

4. Based on steps 1–3, write out a new schedule for yourself and determine any necessary boundaries to make real change possible.

5. Implement a Sabbath practice (a twenty-four-hour window of time you are not "on" and have nothing you are trying to accomplish; a space to be simply human again). View it as an experiment, and keep innovating until you find what works for you!

"Dear Abby," an American advice column in the *San Francisco Chronicle*, has been around since the 1950s. It was started by Pauline Phillips under the pen name Abigail Van Buren. Abigail dished out witty and commonsense advice to the masses, and one of her most famous pieces of advice has become one of my favorites to revisit: "If you want your children to turn out well, spend twice as much time with them, and half as much money."[2]

This is plausibly one of the best parenting tips I've ever come across. It also applies to those who don't currently or may never have children when we consider the same concept for our own wellness.

If you want your soul to be well, spend twice as much time *being* and half as much time *doing*.

Are you tired? Worn out? Burned out on religion? Come to me. Get away with me and you'll recover your life. I'll show you how to take a real rest. Walk with me and work with me—watch how I do it. Learn the unforced rhythms of grace. I won't lay anything heavy or ill-fitting on you. Keep company with me and you'll learn to live freely and lightly. (Matt. 11:28–30 Message)

SOUL CARE PRACTICE NO. 11
Create sustainable rhythms.

Be Radically Honest with Yourself

1. What do you want more of in your life?
2. What do you want to spend less time doing?
3. When are you most at peace, and what keeps you from it regularly?
4. What signals does your body give you to indicate it needs rest and a slower pace?
5. Write out ideal rhythms for your days. How is this different from your current daily routines?

CHAPTER 12

The Question You Should Be Asking

I grew up spending the summers at Tippecanoe Lake in Indiana. One summer my mom and stepdad surprised my stepsisters and me by purchasing a three-seater Jet Ski. I loved it as long as I was in control of the steering and speed. I probably spent four hours a day, every day that the sun was shining, out on that Jet Ski. Sometimes I'd go out in the morning when hardly anyone else was out on the water. The water would be calm, and I'd drive slowly, creating a small V-shaped wave like a flock of geese heading south. Other times I'd hit the gas and hold on tight, creating a ripple of waves. If I was really trying to put on a show or give one of my sisters riding on back a thrill, I'd circle around and go fast over the waves I'd created, making for even choppier waters.

It's fun driving a Jet Ski and zipping around on choppy waters—but it's not always fun being the person on the back of it. It's even worse when you're tubing and being tossed around as you follow in the Jet Ski's chaotic wake.

Like a Jet Ski on water, each of us leaves a wake behind us. The question we should be asking to know what we leave in our wake is simple but requires great vulnerability.

What's it like to be on the other side of me?

It takes a lot of courage to ask that question, so there are other questions you can ask yourself first.

What do I leave behind with my actions and conversations?

How do my spouse, roommate, children, and colleagues at work feel after an interaction with me?

Do I leave people and situations better than I found them?

What is the path I'm cultivating?

If we aren't happy with the answers we come up with, it's an indication that our souls aren't being cared for. I've said it several times already, but nothing matters more than the condition of our souls. They are where everything flows from.

Fruit Is Fact

Back in high school, I dated a guy I thought was amazing for me. Jake was everything I'd ever wanted in a boyfriend: kind, hardworking, and loyal. He made me laugh and occasionally did over-the-top romantic gestures that made me feel like the star in a Nicholas Sparks novel. Like all dating relationships, in the beginning phase I couldn't picture our perfect love story ever coming to an end. After months of dating, however, things began to shift. I spent all my time with Jake, but it never seemed to be enough for him. He got upset with me when I didn't text him back right away, even when it was because I couldn't be on my phone during track practice. My mind was convinced we were good together because he was perfect on paper. Even though I felt more distant from my girlfriends, I had developed such strong feelings for Jake that I kept disregarding my newer, less pleasant feelings about our relationship. Because I let the relationship drag out, things got complicated.

166

I got into fights with Jake because I felt he was too needy. There was drama with my girlfriends because I felt they didn't understand how limited my time was. My mom and I started arguing more, I fell behind on my schoolwork, and my performance on the track team suffered. In hindsight, these things were directly correlated to my relationship with Jake. We stayed together far too long for three reasons. First, I lied to myself: *If you break up with him, you'll regret it.* I told myself, *He'll change, just give it time.* Second, my feelings were confused. I loved my friends and missed them, but I really cared deeply for Jake and didn't want to lose him.

And finally, I didn't pay attention to the fruit of our relationship. Drama with my parents and friends. Inability to perform well at school and in my sport. There was no joy, peace, patience, kindness, goodness, or gentleness oozing out of him or me. The fruit of our relationship was obviously rotten.

Unlike our thoughts or feelings, fruit is fact.

There have been many more times since high school when I haven't paid attention to the fruit and, instead, have allowed my thoughts and feelings to direct my course of action, which is always a mistake.

How often has my mind justified my decision to pull another sleepless night in order to finish a project? My feelings of pride and invincibility cheer me on. But the fruit born from workaholism? An unhealthy, stressed-out, and exhausted Manda with completed yet crummy work. Unripe fruit.

How often have my feelings confused me into staying in a friendship that disrespected my boundaries and left me feeling spent? I talk myself out of having a hard conversation by concentrating on all of the good memories we've had together. But the fruit of toxic friendships? A defeated and annoyed Manda who's increasingly resentful. Moldy fruit.

How often has the lack of wholesome fruit been so glaringly obvious, yet we disregard it because of the reasoning in our minds and our feelings that complicate everything?

After I stopped working at our church to launch my writing career full-time, I committed to serving biweekly in the toddlers' room. I told myself it was the right thing to do, and it felt good to serve. The problem was that whenever I showed up to serve, I was in a crabby mood and wasn't giving the kids or other volunteers my best. I wasn't serving from a place of overflow. Despite my reasoning and motivation, there was no fruit coming from this experience. Even good things, like serving, sometimes need to be cut or put on pause for a while.

This is not to say that if you don't see the result you're hoping for overnight there is no fruit and you should just give up. No; it's quite the opposite, in fact. You won't see the fruit of your labor in many areas of life for years. In foster care specifically, I've realized I will very rarely see the fruit of my labor; however, I don't do it so I can bear witness to its results. It's just a perk when I get to see God make something out of my tiny efforts.

The fruit that I'm talking about here is the fruit of the Spirit: love, joy, peace, patience, kindness, goodness, faithfulness, gentleness, and self-control.

At the start of every new year, my husband and I take time to evaluate and assess our lives under a microscope. We break down our lives by category: friendship, marriage, career, habits, and service to others. As we look at each one, we discuss how we're feeling and what we believe needs intentional change. But the very first thing we do? Consider the fruit.

Friendship Fruit

Certain friendships clearly make me better and produce good fruit. When I'm with these people, and because of the value they add to my life, I experience more love, joy, peace, and so forth. But then there are friendships that are fun (feelings complicate), and we have a long history together (mind justifies), but they don't produce any fruit of the Spirit. Instead, they produce only gossip, envy, and temptation.

As we begin to live conscious, healthy lives in the light, it will become increasingly apparent when someone else isn't. It's vital to count the fruit so we are able to take inventory of the people we surround ourselves with, cut out toxic ones, and create boundaries as needed.

Marriage Fruit

Together with our spouse, are we cultivating more patience, kindness, goodness, and so forth in the world? Are we truly better together? If not, we need to make some changes. Of course, our individual inner health is going to impact our relationship, so that's the first place to investigate.

When Eric and I weren't experiencing much ripe, juicy fruit in our marriage, we knew we needed to figure out why and get to the root cause. It led us to go to counseling, and years later we still go simply as a proactive effort to continue counting the fruit.

Our romantic relationships need to be assessed with candor. Once we identify the fruit or lack thereof, we can pivot and intervene.

Work Fruit

Do we see a return on our investment from our forty-hour workweek, or do we feel like we're wasting our days? Do we need to adjust our attitude because we're the one bringing sour fruit to the conference room? We need to be courageous enough to leave toxic work environments, and we need to be aware enough to do our own inner work too. Every individual either contributes or takes away from a healthy work culture.

Habit Fruit

Spend one week documenting your life (everything you do and for how long), then review it to see your patterns and habits. Here were a few of mine: I turned to food when bored, spent more time on social media than with God, showed up to conversations with intentionality but often gave in to gossip, and prioritized work and fun over God and space. Not only did I have to face such hard facts once I looked back on my week, but I could easily notice what was producing good fruit as well as what was poisoning the soil. Give yourself the gift of full transparency as you notice your habits with food, social media, conversation, sleep, time with God, and more.

Service Fruit

Our good deeds, volunteering, and random acts of kindness should happen out of the overflow of our hearts. If we are doing these things—leading a small group, fostering a child, paying for the person in line behind us—but have a bad attitude or grow resentful, we need to check ourselves. It's crucial to scrutinize our hearts' motives. Especially as followers of Jesus, it's easy to do the right thing for the wrong reasons. God doesn't care about us doing good things or being nice people for our own sake.

Faith Fruit

In response to a pastor we know whose life showed no signs of good fruit, my sweet husband once said, "If reading his Bible is producing that kind of judgment and action in his life, he should stop reading his Bible." While Eric was being facetious, there was some truth to what he said.

If your faith isn't producing the fruit of the Spirit in your life, I'm not saying cut your faith—but pause to consider why that might be. Pay attention. If spending time in prayer, going to church, and reading your Bible aren't softening your heart and leading you to live a life that looks more like Jesus's, something's amiss.

If we aren't seeing the fruit of the Spirit in our lives, we ought to take a good look at the following: Which seeds have been planted, who's watering them, how's the water, and how often are we getting sunlight? How are the seeds of love, joy, peace, patience, kindness, goodness, faithfulness, gentleness, and self-control being planted in us each day? Seeds don't just magically appear; they are gathered and planted by a set of hands. When it comes to fruit of the Spirit, we don't get what we don't seek.

If you aren't tending to your soul and doing the work, how will the seeds ever get watered to grow within you? You can't expect fruit to appear from seeds that are never watered. Is the water that's nourishing the seeds within you purified or diluted? Christians who live and share publicly online will never be able to water your soil the way the Word of God does.

Are you getting enough light? It's not enough to just water the seeds; they need light and warmth to stay alive. If you once experienced a fruit of the Spirit flowing out of you but now it's dwindling (ahem, patience, for me!), then it's time for confession, where everything is brought into the light.

A Word of Caution

You can modify your behavior and try with all your might to be more loving, joyful, peaceful, patient, kind, generous, faithful, gentle, and self-controlled, but the truth is that fruit of the Spirit can't be manufactured, and they certainly won't be sustained through striving. They are the traits that ooze out of a person whose heart, mind, and soul are pursuing God.

I remember being taught the fruit of the Spirit as a child. Despite wonderful intentions, I now recognize that I confused niceness with them and thought being nice was the point of being a Christian. I love what my friend and fellow author Sharon Hodde Miller says in her book *Nice*:

> When confronted with hypocrisy or injustice among fellow Christians, I hemmed and hawed over whether to speak up. What if people got mad? What if people called me names? What if people questioned my motives? Similarly, I was timid with friends who were making destructive decisions. My need to be liked undermined the value of speaking truth, and ultimately, loving them. And so,

too often I went with my backup plan. I selected the option that caused the least amount of waves, the option that didn't require hard conversations and didn't risk any loss. I followed a version of Christianity that actually led me further from Christ.[1]

I'm not saying we shouldn't be nice to each other. But it's easy to pretend to be nice or to choose niceness over the true gospel. It's easy to pat yourself on the back for being nice—but it doesn't equate to fruit. Sometimes niceness can even be an indicator that we are modifying our behavior or acting from a place of self-dependence rather than trusting in God, who calls us to so much more.

What's Inside

During the pandemic, our boys' therapist would come to our home for in-house therapy sessions with each of them every Thursday. Most of the time I used their sessions to get a break from parenting and either work, clean, or numb out on my phone. (Hey, I never said it was the wisest use of my time!)

One Thursday I overheard our teenage son's therapist telling him a story that intrigued me so much that I secretly peered through the staircase railing to witness a powerful lesson being shared.

"Imagine that you are holding a cup of coffee," she said as she handed him a mug with Coca-Cola in it. "And someone comes along and bumps into you, making you spill your coffee everywhere."

She nudged his arm gently and he rolled his eyes.

"Why did you spill your coffee?" she asked him.

"I didn't," he replied, unwilling to tap into imaginary play.

"Pretend for just a second, please."

"Uh, because you bumped into me," he answered.

"Ah! It's interesting, because that's how most people would answer, but I'm going to let you in on a secret even most adults don't know."

My ears perked up. I didn't know where she was going with this.

172

"You spilled coffee because there was coffee in your cup."

He looked at her, confused.

"Had there been water in the cup, you would have spilled water. If there had been Kool-Aid in your cup, you would've spilled Kool-Aid. Whatever is inside the cup is what will spill out," she explained.

Suddenly I knew the point she was demonstrating, and I made a mental note to never forget the example.

"When life comes along and bumps into you—which is bound to happen over and over again to each of us—whatever is inside you will come out," she said.

He nodded as if to understand.

"We have to consider what's in our cup. This way, when life gets tough and bumps into us, we know what is going to spill out."

She offered examples of joy, forgiveness, and peace, then anger, revenge, and anxiety. She explained that the choice of what's in a person's cup is up to them and them alone.

We can dump what's inside when we don't like the thought of it spilling out, through journaling, deep breaths, moving our bodies, and more. We can replace what's inside by making choices we're proud of.

In that moment she taught our teenager a valuable lesson that served as a beautiful reminder for his foster mom too.

Changing What's Inside

As author Wayne W. Dyer says so clearly,

> When you squeeze an orange, you'll always get orange juice to come out. What comes out is what's inside. The same logic applies to you: when someone squeezes you, puts pressure on you, or says something unflattering or critical, and out of you comes anger, hatred, bitterness, tension, depression, or anxiety, that is what's inside. If love and joy are what you want to give and receive, change your life by changing what's inside.[2]

If changing what's inside were easy, there would be no self-help section at the bookstore and far fewer people on medications and in therapy. Changing what's inside is unique to everyone. Some of the things that change what's inside of me and produce good fruit are what I refer to as the "6 Rs": read, rest, reflect, respond, reduce, and receive. If you're not sure where to start, perhaps one or more of these will resonate with you.

Read

Whether it's reading a novel that sucks me in (*Where the Crawdads Sing* was one I couldn't put down), a passage of Scripture (Psalm 139 is a favorite), or a book about someone else's life experience (*I'm Still Here* by Austin Channing Brown was phenomenal), reading changes me. It forces me to slow down, challenges my way of thinking, and teaches me new ways of seeing the world and people.

Rest

I keep saying it because it's true: we were created to be human beings, not human doings. Jesus, God's own Son, who had all the power in the world, napped to rest and withdrew to pray when he lived on this earth and functioned as a human. Who are we to think we don't need rest? Spiritually, physically, and chemically, our bodies need rest to change what's inside.

Reflect

Changing what's inside starts by being *aware* of what's inside. There are so many ways to go about reflection, as noted in the previous chapters. Proper self-reflection leads to self-correction.

Respond

Reacting is instinctual, whereas responding is intentional. When we respond rather than react, it produces good fruit in our relationships and all our interactions.

Many of us do a pretty good job at responding instead of reacting in public. We leave the foolish reaction-based behavior to our toddlers. But we become like a toddler who throws a tantrum and looks like a fool when we're behind a screen. Our technology-addicted generation has developed a bad habit of cultural reactivity. We don't listen before we leap, and it shows. Through jab-filled, unproductive comments online we post just ninety seconds (or less) after reading what someone whom we vehemently disagree with has to say, we throw all manners and common sense out the window. This never helps anyone.

Reacting comes from our gut and is often based on fear and insecurities. Rarely is it the most rational or appropriate way to act. Responding, on the other hand, pauses to consider what the best course of action might be, based on values such as reason, compassion, and cooperation.

The opportunity to react or respond presents itself to us all the time, whether it's our spouse nagging us, our coworker being rude, a friend who said something that really hurt our feelings, or any number of other situations. There will always be external moments that bother us, but if we learn to respond and not just react, we can make things better and not worse.

Reduce

Reducing material things, unwanted commitments, and unhealthy options are one way to change what's inside of ourselves. There is wisdom in getting back to what's essential and courage in cutting out the rest.

Receive

We don't have to do everything on our own or carry heavy times alone. I lean on my people hard when necessary, and as I've learned to receive their help, meals, words of encouragement, and more, I have found that it changes me.

If we aren't seeing the fruit of the Spirit in any area of our lives, that's on us. We need to cut off anything that produces rotten, toxic fruit and spend time with Jesus to experience rich, healthy fruit.

Our minds can lie, and our feelings can confuse us, but fruit produced is undeniably true.

But the fruit of the Spirit is love, joy, peace, forbearance, kindness, goodness, faithfulness, gentleness and self-control. Against such things there is no law. (Gal. 5:22–23)

SOUL CARE PRACTICE NO. 12

Recognize what you leave in your wake.

Be Radically Honest with Yourself

1. Do you spend energy modifying your behavior instead of seeking real transformation?

2. What activities, relationships, and habits aren't serving you anymore?

3. Which fruit of the Spirit would people say they experience from you most?

4. Are you proud of the wake you leave behind?

5. What changes what's inside of you, and do you do this enough?

CHAPTER 13

Recipe for a Life Well Lived

During my time working at Soul City Church, I committed to honoring the staff values. One of the values included a commitment to do more than just maintain. "Stagnancy is the first sign of death," it said. Before then, I'd never really thought about it much, but it made sense. Stagnancy is a state of being immobile and inactive. If we aren't innovating, creating, and pursuing, we can easily become stagnant and complacent in every aspect of our lives: spiritually, physically, and relationally.

The opposite of stagnancy in our lives is not just action or movement. You see, we can stay busy and keep moving without living vibrantly or progressing forward. Even though we might be in motion, our lives are stagnant if our days all look the same and nothing ever changes. Running around like that is how some people spend their entire lives. They don't think they're stagnant, but their souls are dying every day.

Lifelong Learner

I know so many people who never had the opportunity to get to know their grandparents, and even more who don't take time out of their busy schedules to spend it with them. Whenever I've made space to spend quality time with one of my grandparents, I've never regretted it. Grandparents are one of God's greatest treasures to our lives; they impart wisdom, love us through rose-colored lenses, and reveal so much of our family origins. To this day, I spend as much time with my grandma as possible when I'm in town, and since we live thousands of miles apart, we text and video chat often. There's an extra sweetness to hearing baby giggles over live video stream. She's also active on social media, which helps our connection even more. I see my grandma, in many ways, as a lifelong learner. She could say, "That app is too complicated. No thanks!" but instead she asks me to sit down and show her how she can keep up with my writing and photos of our kids by learning how to use it.

When my grandpa, Papaw, retired several years ago, he became noticeably more aloof as days went on. We were all worried about his mental and physical health. Thankfully, my grandma talked him into getting a part-time job at a local, super-friendly grocery store just to get him out of the house, keep his mind active, and boost his spirits as he regained human interaction. I really believe this is what gave us a couple of extra years with him. Sadly, when Papaw's physical health dramatically declined, he couldn't do his job anymore. It wasn't long after he was stuck in a chair all day, every day, that his mental health followed suit and declined as well. Our whole family endured the tremendously difficult loss of him right after Christmas that year.

My husband's grandparents have had an entirely different experience through retirement. They don't spend much time in front of the TV or eat unhealthy processed snacks all day. Instead of using their old age as a free pass for bad habits, they use it as all the more reason to pursue health. "I'm too old for that" would never come out of their mouths. They book trips, volunteer in classrooms, take up new hobbies, and learn new skills. While there are many factors to a person's health, I really believe that they are thriving at well over eighty years of age because they aren't stagnant. They are constantly learning, using their gifts, and looking for ways to positively impact the world—ingredients for a life well lived.

Upside-Down Kingdom

Have you ever thought about what you'd do if it were your very last day on earth? I know it sounds morbid, but just go there with me. What would you do? Who would you want to be with? How would you spend your precious final 720 minutes?

> Go skydiving.
> Enjoy the best meal with your favorite people.
> Give all you have to the poor.
> Hold your kids tight.
> Fly to your dream destination.
> Make peace with somebody.

These are some of the answers I found online and received when I surveyed a few friends. They're not bad. In fact, they reveal that we value adventure, beauty, generosity, quality time, and love.

However, none of us know when our last day will be, so why wouldn't we live like this today? I haven't been able to shake this thought.

If you died tomorrow, how do you think you would be remembered?

Would others talk about how you never tried new things because of fear or how you always said yes to adventure? Would people reminisce about how you were such a workaholic or the beautiful ways you prioritized people over productivity? Would you be known as someone who held all of your money and possessions closely or as someone who gave freely?

There is a real disconnect between how I would spend my last day on earth and the life I am presently living.

I would spend my last day on earth serving everyone I know. I would forgo my Netflix shows, social media scrolling, and attempts to capture the perfect picture. I would not freak out about my husband's driving and would let go of any grudges I'm holding. I wouldn't rush out the door without saying "I love you." I wouldn't spend another penny on myself when I could instead invest in someone who needs a place to lay their head more than I need another iced latte.

The truth is that most days I spend more time online and meaningless pursuits than I do serving others. But I want to be remembered for more than the clothes I wore or the pictures and captions I shared. I want to serve the people who live under my roof and my whole community.

What I know for sure is this: Jesus was fully aware when it was his final day on earth, and he spent it washing feet. Washing feet. What if that is the recipe to a life well lived?

What's Holding You Back?

Why is it that we talk ourselves out of learning, using our gifts, or positively impacting the world? Far more than I'd like to admit, I talk myself out of trying something new in fear of embarrassment, failure, and wasted time. Thinking I'm too old or that it'll take too long are two of the lies that hold me back from learning. Unlike my husband's grandparents, who decide they want to learn something and then go after it, I tend to make excuses and let fear dictate my choices. Whether it's learning how to play the piano, speak French, ballroom dance, or sew, who put an age limit on these things? So what if it takes a year or more? What else would you be doing with that time? Even if you never become proficient, fluent, or elite, there is so much value in learning new things.

I've started to realize that the more I learn, the less I know. Keeping an open mind and soft heart are part of the beginner's process. There is no better time than now to learn something new. If we want to live abundant lives, we've got to stop underestimating the power of learning. We have to embrace being a first-timer as often as possible.

I talk myself out of using my gifts mostly in fear of what other people think, and sometimes because of imposter syndrome. I've started recognizing that the little voice whispering, *Who are you to teach about that?* or *No one cares what you have to say*, gets louder as I get closer to the very thing I'm supposed to be doing. No longer do those lies hold me back, because I view them as obnoxious neon signs screaming THIS WAY! KEEP GOING! PEOPLE NEED THIS! IT'S A BRIGHT LIE AND THE ENEMY IS AFRAID.

Getting over the fear of what people think so that we use our gifts is easier than we might think. When your identity is rooted in truth and no longer changes based on your performance or the opinions of others, you can stop avoiding things that otherwise would be threatening. For example, when my identity is secure, I can use my gift as a writer unabashedly, because even when someone shares their opinion that I'm an awful writer and they don't like my work, my identity is unfazed. Sure, my feelings may get hurt temporarily, but I'm not going to throw in the towel on writing altogether. Why? Because I am so much more than a writer, and I'm not writing to please everyone.

When we become selfish, we don't positively impact the world. It's selfish to spend our days focused only on ourselves and the people in our little bubble. There is so much more to this life than having a big house with a security system, extra zeros at the end of our bank statement, or the perfect family photos. We're hungry for a life that's meaningful, yet so many of us chase the American Dream, settling for a life that's devoted to ourselves. Why do you think so many people who "have it all" aren't happy? Happiness isn't the result of having everything we ever wanted. Happiness is what we experience as we give all we have to each other.

We can't possibly impact the world for good if we're complacent. Complacency happens when we embrace mediocrity as a way of life. It deprives us of opportunities and brings our growth to a standstill. When we're complacent, we have no motivation to push for better. We stop developing ourselves and become obsolete. Complacency is often a root cause of a failed career, a divorce, or a severed friendship. Not a single good thing comes from complacency. If we want to not waste our lives, we're going to have to live deliberately in pursuit of growth for the benefit of all.

Stay

What drives you to escape or to feel the longing to escape in your life? Another way to consider this question: What makes you want to quit your life, take off, and start over?

For me, it's feeling trapped, overwhelmed, or hopeless.

What is it for you? Conflict? Discomfort? Being known intimately?

The beauty in being aware of what drives us to escape is that it shows us where we need God most. When we are aware, we can fight our desire to take flight. We can choose to stay. To not escape—through alcohol, excessive shopping, or hiding under the covers—and instead stay in the reality of our densely layered lives while God meets us in our desperation.

Honor Your Growth

Most ingredients to a life well lived are wrapped in forward motion, but reflection and appreciation are equally important. We must take the time and space to be proud of how far we've come. That is how we appreciate the lives we're living. Even though doing so may not seem very exciting, it cannot be undervalued.

Notice moments when you handle a situation better than a previous, less healthy version of yourself would have been able to. Did you say no to an invitation that your inner people-pleaser would have said yes to previously? Did you respond in a heated moment with your child instead of reacting? Did you confess something that your former self would have buried in shame?

Honor your growth by celebrating how caring for your soul is working to reshape you for the better.

Life Motto

During our seven-month engagement, Eric and I began to think about a motto to build our lives around. We felt it was important to be clear about the purpose of our marriage and intentional with our days, since no one knows how many they have left. We don't recall where we first heard it or who said it, but the phrase we chose is, "When you have more than you need, build a longer table, not a higher fence." We wanted a motto we could take into consideration and measure our decisions against that would never expire, and this was it.

We then broke it down to clarify what it would mean for our lives on a daily basis. First, we defined what it meant to have more than we need, and we soon realized that we had abundantly more than we needed. In fact, we had all of our needs covered, and just about every single want as well. We had each other, loving families, friends, connections, food in our fridge, and never a second thought about how we'd pay our bills. I once heard that no one ever gets poor by giving too much, and we've been putting it to the test. We give of our time, money, energy, and resources. We give to the point where we feel it, because anything less isn't actually generosity.

Next, we defined what it meant for us to build a longer table, which could mean a lot of different things. We agreed it was about making room for more people to enjoy our abundance and

183

widening our perspective on life. We knew the building part would require some intentional work on our end. So we became foster parents, read books by authors of color, and opened our laundry room to people without a washer and dryer to use. We sought opportunities to share our food, our vehicle, our spare bedroom, our network, and our love. At first, that's what having a longer table was all about for us: spending our privilege and "extra" well. Now, it's more about sharing what we have and receiving gifts we didn't even know to ask for. Gifts such as children and parents we get to partner with for a season, friends who have a different sexual orientation from us, and stereotypes being dismantled right before our eyes. Gifts of seeing new angles on politics, tasting the goodness that is Popeye's chicken, and having the most beautiful moments that make me think, *We could've missed this.*

Lastly, we defined what a higher fence meant to us, so that we could always check ourselves. A higher fence, we decided, was accumulating more and widening the gap between ourselves and others. We began to consider every decision we made in light of the reality that we're always building either a longer table or a higher fence. If something we choose keeps us further from people who don't look like us, it's a fence. If it doesn't challenge stereotypes of groups of people, it's an even higher fence.

Building a longer table, on the other hand, is about putting some of our wants aside so that others' needs can be met. This includes our finances but extends far beyond that. It doesn't just mean buying more food—in fact, as you welcome more people and their needs into your life, you'll be amazed at the abundance that follows. They'll bring you lasagna and laughter, wine and wacky stories. Building a longer table is choosing to make space for more people and valuing them as equals despite your differences.

I think the reason we sometimes build fences and cling to what we have is because we worked so hard to get it. I used to have a hard time with generosity. I gave only when specific conditions were met. I believed that because I worked so hard to earn my living, it was mine. This is where my faith really cramps my style sometimes. In Acts 20:34–35, Paul explains that one of the goals of our hard work paying off is so that we can share the reward by helping others:

> You yourselves know that these hands of mine have supplied my own needs and the needs of my companions. In everything I did, I showed you that by this kind of hard work we must help the weak, remembering the words the Lord Jesus himself said: "It is more blessed to give than to receive."

Building a longer table is what God did for us by putting Jesus in the flesh on earth. It just so happens that Jesus was a carpenter who could literally build tables. He made a place at the table for people his own society rejected. Oh, the irony! Jesus could have built a higher fence but instead tore the old fence down. The law of the Old Testament excluded so many, so the cross Jesus died on became symbolic of a table that makes room for everyone to come and feast with God.

When we make room for others, we make room for Jesus.

Eric and I haven't always seen perfectly eye to eye when it comes to our faith. There have been seasons when one of us wasn't as sure about the Bible, if I'm honest. But we are certain that the documented life of Jesus is the best model to follow. After all, we couldn't possibly believe that God only brought us together for our personal happiness and great sex—although both are lovely. It had to be about so much more. We've lived into that. As husband and wife, we can do more to help bring heaven to earth by following Jesus together.

However, bringing heaven to earth doesn't happen without some seriously intentional living.

Every Day on Purpose

It's tempting to get comfortable and just live a life of ease. Some days I find the temptation so strong that I indulge in a package of Oreos and a good show on Hulu. I numb out, avoiding my problems. If these are isolated incidents, I'll be OK, as long as I am aware enough to not make it a habit. However, if numbing out becomes the reality of my days on repeat, it won't be long before I wake up one day and ask what the heck I've done to better the world in the last five years.

Stagnancy runs much deeper than Oreos and binge-watching. This is about a whole life spent seeking comfort and ease. It's about day after day looking the same. It's about being afraid to look inward, question who you are, and consider why you believe what you believe. Now, I'm not saying you have to be a nomad and live out of your van in order to avoid stagnancy (although I'm sure such people have a lot of interesting things to add from their perspective).

The scariest part of living stagnant is that some people don't believe there's anything wrong with it. I want to grab them by the shoulders, look them in the eye, and say, "God formed your life through a series of divine and scientific miracles. Your mother's body went through the wringer just to get you here. You have unique gifts and talents and purpose. Don't waste your life!"

The good news is that if you find yourself stuck or in a life that's stagnant, you have the power to change that.

Assess Your Life Continually

Assessing your life doesn't have to be a long, drawn-out process. It can be as simple as answering a couple of questions honestly each week and assessing a bit more thoroughly once each quarter. Ask yourself the following questions:

1. Who is teaching me something new, and what have I learned?
2. Where do I need to innovate?
3. When did I rest well this week?

4. Why am I not [insert whatever you're avoiding]?

5. How have I stepped out of my comfort zone?

Ask for Feedback Regularly

If you want to live a life that's moving forward, you're going to have to get comfortable with being uncomfortable. Remember that star on the mall directory that says, "You are here"? You've got to figure out where you are before you can get to where you want to go.

Determining where you are requires intentional conversations with people in your life whom you trust to give honest feedback. Send someone who really knows you the following questions, and see if they'd be willing to sit down and share their answers with you:

1. What do I do that inspires you?

2. What do I do that bothers you?

3. What do I not know about myself?

4. How am I cultivating influence?

5. How am I not cultivating influence or even losing influence?

When I asked one of my older friends whom I admire a lot to provide feedback for me, she was so honored I asked. We met up in person, and I wasn't surprised by her answer to the second question. "It bothers me when you lose your cool over seemingly small things," she said. "You could work on maintaining your composure in stress."

I nodded as the words came out of her mouth. *That bothers me too!* I thought. *Could this be another area of transformation for me, rather than writing it off or accepting it as my genetics?*

Her response to the third question brought tears to my eyes instantly. "Manda, I don't know if you know that you are fun . . .

that people really enjoy being around you. Not just because you are great at so many things but simply for who you are as a person. You're actually fun to be around, but I don't think you realize that's why people want to spend time with you."

This triggered something within me, and I couldn't stop the tears from welling up. Tears are always something to pay attention to, so I later spoke about this with my counselor, who helped me see that somewhere in my life, I was made to believe I wasn't fun. Sadly, I had been living as if I had something to offer in relationships but it just wasn't "fun."

Her response to the fifth question allowed me to see my addiction to productivity more clearly. "Manda, you might be losing influence because you're always a driver, never a player. You drive by staying so focused on work and tackling challenges ahead of you, but you rarely let loose and interact with others without an agenda behind it. While you are so great at driving change in the world, you might be surprised at how your influence will expand if you make space to play more."

It dawned on me how true everything was that she shared. Most people are terrified of feedback because they think it's going to be all negative, but in my experience, I receive far more on the encouragement side! You too can experience growth instead of complacency by choosing courage and asking for feedback regularly.

Be More Afraid of Staying the Same

Quite possibly the best way to stop living a life that's stagnant is to become more afraid of staying the same than you are of taking steps forward. Start envisioning a life where nothing changes and you die without having done anything beyond what you did today. Does the thought make you squirm a little bit in your seat? Now picture your career or your marriage ten years from now. Do you honestly see them lasting and flourishing if you simply maintain how they are right now in this very moment?

It helps to picture what a future without growth and intentionality looks like because it scares us, and as long as the fear of staying put outweighs the fear of moving forward, we won't be at risk for stagnancy.

You can avoid ruffling feathers by always keeping your mouth shut. You can avoid feeling uncomfortable by staying in your own little bubble. You can avoid having your efforts criticized by doing nothing at all. But to live a life that isn't stagnant, you can't avoid those things any longer.

Don't you dare live the same life for sixty years and call it good. Please, I'm begging you. Don't waste your life. Let's get serious about our evolution and renewal—especially as followers of Jesus. Our transformation and the way we spend our lives is our greatest testimony.

We want each of you to show this same diligence to the very end, so that what you hope for may be fully realized. We do not want you to become lazy, but to imitate those who through faith and patience inherit what has been promised. (Heb. 6:11–12)

SOUL CARE PRACTICE NO. 13
Become insatiably curious.

Be Radically Honest with Yourself

1. If everything stayed the same about your life, ten years from now what would you be happy about? What would disappoint you?

2. Which area of your life is stagnant?

3. Write a life motto for yourself. What needs to change so you can live it out intentionally?

4. How do you talk yourself out of using your gifts or stepping out of your comfort zone?

5. Who do you trust, and have relational equity with, to seek feedback from regularly?

CHAPTER 14

Growth Doesn't Happen by Accident

I ran track in college and am an Enneagram 8 who tends to have more confidence in her abilities than she should, so I didn't think it would be a huge deal to sign up for the Chicago marathon at the last minute. To my surprise, other people had been training for over six months by the time I decided to run 26.2 miles alongside them in the crisp October air.

Eric told me that if I wanted to avoid an injury, I would need to train well. As the days and weeks went on, he would ask me, "When are you going to start training consistently, babe?" which really bugged me. I was running a couple of miles here and there, and adrenaline would carry me the day of, I assured him.

Then the day of the marathon arrived, and my nerves kicked in. I wanted to do well, and for me that meant finishing in less than five hours.

While I was able to finish, it took me over five hours and it wasn't pretty. I peed my pants numerous times (proof I was at least hydrated) and genuinely thought I might die at multiple points along the way (from mile 19 to the finish line, specifically).

The next day disappointment settled in. I'd wanted to do better. But the reality was I hadn't been willing to do what it took to run a marathon in under five hours. I hadn't been willing to put in the hours of training every day. I left it to chance, and my performance showed it.

McDonald's and Oreos

It makes sense that one minute I'm talking about running a marathon while the next I'm on to McDonald's and Oreos. You see, to know me is to know that I love working out and loathe eating healthy.

More times than I can count, I've declared that this was going to be the year I eliminate McDonald's and Oreos from my diet. For me, it's never been about losing weight but rather about my health overall. I know I need to make more nutritious choices when it comes to my diet, but I've struggled to follow through.

The question isn't if I *want* to change my diet. The question is if I'm *willing* to change my diet.

Maybe you want to get a solid eight hours of sleep each night or start a blog. Perhaps you want to exercise at least four times each week or learn ASL. It could be that you want to pay off all your student loan debt in the next three years or quit drinking. Why is it that we don't go after these things we so badly want? I probably didn't name the specific thing you want, but honestly, I care more about why you aren't going after it than the actual thing itself.

Do you think you can't achieve it? Are you unsure of how to begin? Do you lack the time or resources? Sometimes there are legitimate reasons for why we aren't going after our dreams and desires, but more often I think it's because we aren't willing to put in the work.

Here's the truth: you are already really good at being willing. Think about it this way: you go to work not because you want to but because you're willing to do what it takes to put food on the table. You pay your bills not because you want to but because you're willing to do what it takes to have comforts and luxuries in your life. You do the laundry not because you want to but because you're willing to put in the effort so your clothes don't stink. This is true in big and small things alike. No matter how tired I am at the end of the night, I wash my makeup off not because I want to but because I'm willing to do what it takes to prevent breakouts and wrinkles.

If we aren't doing something we want to do, it's a matter of willingness. No one gets what they want without being willing to do something about it. No one coasts into skills or success or growth.

I love the way my pastor Jarrett Stevens put this in the form of a question: "Are you willing to do what only you can do for the things that matter most?"[1]

What's a specific area in your life in which you want to see change but haven't been willing to put in the work? Instead of just repeatedly thinking, *I want to* _____, start following that up with, *So I'm willing to* _____.

A few years ago, I did this and shared it publicly. I wanted more space and rest in my life, so I had to be willing to say no to a bunch of people and opportunities that kept me overly busy. Before that year, I'd complained about being stressed out and overscheduled but never did anything to change it. Once I identified what it would take to change and determined I was willing to try it, I began to experience real transformation.

The Condition of Your Soul

There are plenty of books, people, and other resources that exist to help you identify your goals and chase your dreams. I hope this one motivates you to think outside of the box and gives you permission to get after it—but not at the price of your soul.

You could be wildly successful in your career, achieve all your fitness goals, have more money in your bank account than you know what to do with, and still be unhappy. Why? How could that be?

Because the condition of your soul matters more than anything else.

How often do we get this backward? We work on our appearances and other practicalities of life, paying attention to our souls only if there is time left over. You know the drill: finish the work, lose the weight, clean the house, cook the meal . . .

We are overly focused on outward things, and it skews our priorities. Then we wonder why we're so unhappy and exhausted.

If we pay attention to our souls with only our leftover time and space, we'll quickly trip over the truth: there is no such thing as leftover time or space! We need to flip the script.

What if we prioritized being conscious of our character as much as we prioritize completing tasks? What if we started worrying more about not losing our spouse than losing a few extra pounds? What if we worked on healing the things we like to keep secret instead of hiding them?

I'll tell you because I'm living it: spiritual growth is what happens when we concentrate and care for our souls.

Spiritual Growth

Spiritual growth is the process of becoming more and more like Jesus. When we place our faith in God, the Holy Spirit begins the process of making us more like him, which means we begin to make less sense to the world.

When this happens, we may have peace when there is no logical reason to have anything but anxiety. We might forgive and be gracious when those who don't know Jesus would hold a grudge and be harsh. We hopefully become people who give away more and more of our resources, trusting in God's abundance and faithfulness even in uncertain times.

Spiritual growth is best identified by the fruit of the Spirit be-coming increasingly evident in our lives. Spiritual growth and transformation go hand in hand. We can't grow spiritually without transforming who we are, and we can't transform without growth. Spiritual growth happens when our intentional efforts and the Holy Spirit are actively in collaboration. Only with both of those things can we overcome sin and steadily become more like Jesus. The number of people who message me asking how to grow in their relationship with God, how to pray, or how to remedy their unbelief seems to be increasing by the day.

They ask how, but most already know the answer. First, that there isn't really an answer at all; our spiritual lives are more ab-stract than that. Second, that it would require something of them they aren't willing to hand over quite yet.

At some point in our journey with God, we have to surrender our control, pride, certainty, time, habits, excuses, comfort, and more. We shouldn't be asking how. Instead, we need to ask our-selves, *Am I willing?*

Instead of willing ourselves to be closer to God, be more at-tuned with the Spirit, or live a life that looks more like Jesus's, we have to be willing to surrender. Surrendering means acknowledging that we can't be our own hero. While many self-help books out there will tell us that we don't need a hero because we are our own heroes, I call that baloney.

You're amazing, but you can't save your own soul. Surrender-ing means being open to receiving God's direction and authority over your life. You may hear that you should harness the life you want with reckless abandon, but I have to burst your bubble and remind you that God's plan for your life is so much better than anything you could ever dream up.

Surrendering means following through on the convictions we receive. Sometimes following our convictions looks like walking away from a pattern in our lifestyles such as gossip or gluttony. Other times following through on our convictions will require us to speak up or make a career change. The good news is that if we act upon our convictions but later believe we "heard God wrong," we won't mess up his plans. None of us are that powerful.

Not by Accident

Growth isn't something we're just going to stumble into. We aren't going to wake up one day healed, whole, free, light, and secure. No, these are things we can only experience as we do the inner work and pursue a relationship with our Maker.

Our continued growth is vital. Any muscles that aren't strengthened intentionally will become weak. We see this with a lot of leaders taking a public fall nowadays. Men and women who have accomplished such amazing things for the world and the kingdom of God are facing public humiliation because they neglected to care for their souls. There is truly nothing sadder to me than a person whose gifts take them where their character can't sustain them.

I am the vine; you are the branches. If you remain in me and I in you, you will bear much fruit; apart from me you can do nothing. (John 15:5)

SOUL CARE PRACTICE NO. 14

Match your will with your want.

Be Radically Honest with Yourself

1. What do you leave to chance instead of intentionally acting on?

2. What do you want, and are you willing to make the sacrifices to see it come to fruition?

3. How is the condition of your soul?

4. Do you feel the need to be your own hero or savior? What might change if you surrendered?

5. What is one step you will take to pursue growth going forward?

CHAPTER 15

Turn the Lights On

In a world where we are taught to put our best face forward, it's no surprise that many seem to hit their breaking point without warning. On the outside they seem to have it all together, but on the inside they are dying . . . literally. According to the American Foundation for Suicide Prevention, there is an average of 132 suicides per day in America.[1] Every single day 132 lives are lost to mental health struggles and the pressure to prove; mine was almost one of them.

We share, tweet, 'gram, boast, do, and impress—meanwhile, things are actually falling apart. The pressure to prove ourselves is so great that we slip into the habit of small fabrications that seem like innocent interactions and shortcut our way around until we're lost in the dark. Then shame does its very worst work to keep us there.

On the outside, it's a divorce, midlife crisis, or suicide no one ever saw coming. Shocked when the truth comes out, we wonder how we never noticed. How could our friend and loved one have been in such a dark place, yet we didn't even know? We mourn the loss, but the damage is done. We wish we could have helped prevent it.

Maybe we can. By living transparent lives in the light, free of impressing, not only do we experience freedom for ourselves but we free others too.

What It Means to Be Rich

When we first moved to Los Angeles, I was intimidated by a few of our neighbors. One is a costume designer for a super popular TV show, another is an insanely talented up-and-coming singer-songwriter, and the one who shares walls with us upstairs is a famous social media personality with over two million people consistently watching his content on YouTube, TikTok, and Instagram. From what I could see, each of them appeared to be well known, wealthy, and outrageously successful in their lane.

It didn't take long for me and Eric to get to know them. We always do our best to go out of our way to interact with our neighbors, even if it's just a short chat in the elevator. Once we got into a rhythm of spending our evenings on the rooftop of our condo building, watching the sunset each night, we made sure to invite them. It wasn't formal, just a simple, "Hey, if you want to join us on the rooftop, we go up there around sunset most nights. Feel free to come hang!" Honestly, I didn't think any of them would come. I assumed they had better things to do than spend an evening with us, an ordinary, obscure married couple who also happened to be parents.

What could we possibly have to offer them? They have it all.

Much to my surprise, our neighbors joined us. Time and time again, they showed up on the rooftop. And it wasn't long before my feelings of inadequacy faded. It was through some of the most raw, heartfelt conversations with our neighbors that I was reminded money can't buy happiness, and success alone won't satisfy your soul.

Money has made their lives easier but certainly hasn't made them happier. Although it can provide them the vehicle of their dreams and the ability to get an acai bowl every day without a second thought of whether it's in the budget, it can't buy them the very things they need and desperately ache for:

True friends whose intentions are pure.

Families who support their dreams.

Being seen, known, and loved for who they are, not what they do.

Less stress.

More time to enjoy life.

On the opposite end of the spectrum, my day job in LA is working with my unhoused neighbors, aka people experiencing homelessness. These people don't have money and lack nearly every material possession, yet some of them are a different kind of happy I rarely experience. Skid Row (the sixteen-plus blocks of condensed homelessness in Los Angeles) is dirty, trauma filled, and heartbreaking in so many ways. It's also a place, like most developing countries I've visited, where I am reminded that people can be so poor yet so rich in a different currency. The currency of community, connection, and contentment.

No One Is Immune

Anthony Bourdain, one of the world's most famous chefs and TV personalities, died by suicide at age sixty-one. Iconic fashion designer Kate Spade died by suicide in her New York City high-rise at age fifty-five. A four-time Olympic gold medalist known as the greatest gymnast of all time, Simone Biles, withdrew from Olympic competition for the sake of her mental health at age twenty-four.

By now everyone is aware that no one is immune to depression. Mental health struggles aren't dependent upon age, gender, sexual orientation, economic status, religious beliefs, or social media following. Mental health does not discriminate.

One day I opened an app expecting squares of joy, humor, and wisdom from friends and strangers I enjoy following, but on this day I was met with devastating news. My whole body froze, and I let out an audible shriek. Moments later my three boys walked through the front door, arriving home from school, and saw me tucked up in one of the gray chairs in our front living room, staring at my phone with my jaw hanging low. Tears began to fill my eyes as I read and reread the caption beneath my cyber-friend's posted image. *It couldn't be. There's no way. This isn't real. What's happening?* She was letting the world know her husband had died by suicide the night prior. It was a shock to my system. They were an adorable couple around the same age as me and Eric. A beautiful family, they both worked tirelessly for the good of others and were deeply involved in the local church. Just twelve hours ago I'd watched video footage of him laughing and playing with their sons via Instagram stories.

How could he be gone? What changed in those twelve hours? I couldn't wrap my brain around it. As my mind pondered how his wife and sons were probably feeling, I wept.

Many people who never know or share that they have depression die by suicide. But this man's death came as a shock not because he never talked about his struggle but because he *did*. He was open about his hardships and his ongoing battle against depression, and I always admired that about him. From what I saw and heard, this man did everything you're supposed to do: see a doctor, take medication, go to therapy, bring struggles into the light, and stay far from isolation.

The truth is that maybe nothing happened in those twelve hours. Most suicides aren't caused by one event. Someone who attempts or dies by suicide has struggled for a long period of time. The current crisis may have been triggered by a particular event, but only someone who is *already* in deep distress considers such an extreme reaction.[2]

His death was an eye-opener. Not one of us is immune to the dark, to unhealthiness, or to mistakes that bury us in shame. Every time I hear of another person dying by suicide—and it's far more often than I can bear—I wonder what kind of mental and soul illness they were warring with.

I hope you know there is nothing you could ever do that would make you better off dead. There is no flaw, shadow, or sin within you that God can't transform. He longs to heal you. He wants to set you free and see you living whole.

Fuel or Firehose

One day my thirteen-year-old foster son, Goof, and I sat waiting in our agency's holding room for an hour past his scheduled visitation appointment time.

Without any words and with my eyes fixated on the entrance door, I prayed his mom would show up. Thirty minutes into our wait, I felt myself getting annoyed and angry. I watched as my son grew bored and agitated. I started praying for patience and grace. When fifteen more minutes passed, I moved on to praying for guidance if she didn't show. I knew what was likely going to happen, because it had happened before; he would grieve, and it would come out in the form of hate toward all of us who just want to love him.

God, equip me to comfort him far beyond my own ability. I repeated it over and over: *Equip me.*

Alas, she was deemed a no-show. We said goodbye to our caseworker and headed home—his Mother's Day gift still in hand. Although he tried to hide it, I could tell he was crushed. He pulled his hood up, stared out the window, and fought back tears as we drove home in silence. Seeing him hurt made my heart hurt.

When he finally decided to talk, he let loose—saying negative things, calling names, and expressing that he "knew it was gonna happen."

I had a choice in how to respond.

Naturally, I wanted to chime in and affirm my son. It *is* selfish that she would confirm only a few hours prior and then just not show. It *is* unfair that we waited and didn't receive even a simple courtesy call. It *is* wrong that promises are being made and never kept. *No one* deserves this, let alone a child.

But God.

(It's annoying when God makes us more like him, isn't it?) Before I could open my mouth, the Spirit interrupted with a thought. *His house is on fire, Manda. What are you going to do? Add fuel to the flames, or hose it down?*

I was meant to illustrate love and grace by being a peacemaker. This does not come naturally for me. I'm a fighter, a disrupter, and an advocate. But I swallowed my pride and followed the Spirit's prompting. I needed to be the firehose, not the fuel.

Our resulting conversation was one where God was speaking, and I was just the mouthpiece for what he wanted my boy to hear. I affirmed Goof's feelings and assured him that children aren't supposed to be the ones waiting for their parents to show up. And then we discussed the reality that, in his case, things may never change, but that he had the power to decide how much he let it affect him. Goof told me that someday, if he became a father, he would never do that to his kid.

We drove the rest of the way home in silence, because there wasn't much else I could say that wouldn't add fuel to his fire. And what typically would have been a terrible evening, based on other no-show visitations, miraculously ended up being a night to remember for all of the good it contained. Our son asked to make us dinner (nachos, his favorite) and to play Monopoly as a family. (Clearly God still hadn't answered my prayer to change his favorite board game to a much shorter one yet.) We laughed and he smiled—there was a lightness in the air.

Later, when I tucked him in for bed, he asked me to lie next to him and rub his back. I did and felt nostalgic. *Just like Mom used to do for me.*

While we lay there in silence, only a sliver of light pouring in from the hallway onto his soft cheeks, I prayed again. Eyes open, no words spoken aloud. Just conversing with God in thought.

God gave me this vision of Goof's house a second time. This time there were no flames, just smoke, as if the fire had recently been put out. Once I could tell he was asleep, I quietly tiptoed out of his room, and paused one last time before closing the door. I looked in at this precious boy, hurting and healing all at once, and I whispered, "We're going to rebuild the house, buddy. One way or another, we're going to rebuild your house. Don't worry. Love you."

Just as the door closed, I heard him sleepily mutter, "Love you too."

Turn the Lights On

In that moment I realized we had put out the fire and turned the lights back on. Turning the lights on means paying attention. *What are the people around me going through?* It means listening to the Spirit of God and doing what doesn't always feel natural or like the sensible thing.

Turning the lights on means doing something when someone's house is on fire instead of ignoring it. *Am I willing to help, maybe even be inconvenienced?* More simply, turning the lights on requires the obedience to act upon the answer to the question "What would Jesus do?"

This applies in simple, everyday situations, such as when people are gossiping and you have a choice to stay in the dark by chiming in or turn the lights on by changing the subject. And when we read an opposing view online and decide to comment, we can do so in a manner that either adds fuel to the flames or puts the fire out. Perhaps this consideration leads us to keep our clickety-clacking fingers away from the keyboard and the comment to ourselves altogether.

If we are in a situation where we witness someone being excluded or ignored, we can turn the lights on by choosing to include and acknowledge them. Don't overthink it. Remember how I mentioned earlier that embracing embarrassment for the sake of freedom is good for your soul? Risking embarrassment for the sake of another human being's wellness is equally good for your soul—and the universe at large.

Rewrite False, Negative Scripts

Sometimes the lights get turned off by other people, even those who are supposed to be safe and loving caretakers who keep the lights on.

When my friend Melissa was in the second grade, she failed her eye exam. She went home and told her parents, handing them the slip saying they needed to take her to an eye doctor for prescription glasses. Her mom accused her of failing the eye exam on purpose and told her that she wanted glasses for attention. Melissa was confused and lived with extremely blurry vision for another year. Unfortunately, this created a false script that replayed in her mind: *My needs don't matter.*

As the years went on, Melissa's false belief that her needs didn't matter led her to consistently put herself last and neglect her needs. After hitting rock bottom in an entirely different way than I did, she knew it was time to write a new script full of truth and believe it in order to heal: *I matter. My needs are real, and they matter. I am worthy of being cared for by myself and cared about by others.*

I have another friend who grew up being told both directly and indirectly: *Trust no one. Everyone will stab you in the back. No one truly cares. You're on your own.* She lived this script out so deeply that she was hardwired to look for the worst in everyone and every scenario. She spent a good portion of her life in isolation without friends, skeptical of all interactions.

When I asked her how she healed and turned the lights on, she told me that God led her to people who proved they were trustworthy and revealed to her which ones had good intentions and were worthy of being trusted. She said the work to rewrite the script ingrained in her is daily, even hourly. She talks to herself to silence her inner critic and the lies that creep up. When someone shares something positive and kind about her, she said it's still hard to believe, but she now accepts it and repeats it to herself until it feels real and believable. Over time, her negative and false scripts are being rewritten, and she's healing. She has friends she trusts and leans on. Her life is infinitely brighter and lighter.

What was caught or taught to you as a child? Is there a negative script you replay in your mind or that lives deep in your soul? What is a truthful affirmation you can begin to speak over yourself to rewrite it and turn the lights on?

Let Your Light Shine

You know that feeling when you discover something awesome for the first time? Like the next best thing since sliced bread? That thing you literally cannot keep to yourself?

For me, this has happened a number of times:

- When I first learned that the Chicken Shop (an incredible spot in the West Loop of Chicago) has 50 percent off every Monday night if you simply mention you have the app on your phone.
- When I first tasted the fettuccine chicken alfredo from The Pasta Bowl.
- When I first learned how to chill my wine without watering it down. Two words: frozen grapes.
- When I first found out, during one of our moves, that you can transition your clothes on their hangers, without them all falling everywhere, if you simply put a trash bag around the bottom of them.

- When a friend showed me how to light hard-to-reach candle wicks by using a strand of raw spaghetti.
- When a lady in a shoe store taught me how to use pieces of pool noodle to keep my boots wrinkle-free and upright in my closet.

If you're anything like me, you can't contain your excitement and knowledge about really cool life hacks. When something adds value to our lives, we naturally want to spread the word.

This is why the very best marketing plan is not to spend thousands of dollars on advertising a product that's subpar but rather to create a product people will not want to stop talking about. Anyway, back to my point: people share what they love or what's changed their lives for the better.

That's precisely why I wrote this book, friend. (I figure it's OK to call you that, now that we've come this far.) I've experienced what life is like when my soul is well tended, and I cannot go back. I've experienced what's on the other side of impressing: freedom. I've found hope and new reasons to live. I've experienced wholeness, and I long for every single person I meet to experience it for themselves. God flipped a switch in me, and ever since, I've refused to dim the light or turn it off for anyone. I've also learned that staying in the light is a lifelong practice.

Stay in the Light

Every Sunday night, Eric and I ask each other the same three questions:

1. How have I loved you well this week?
2. Is there anything you've been feeling guilty or convicted about that you need to confess or discuss?
3. How can I best support you in this coming week?

Most Sunday nights end really well because of the discussions that come from these intentional conversations. However, I'd be lying if I told you these questions always go well. The reality is that asking them sometimes leads to a fight where I storm out of the room yelling or Eric shuts down. These questions require us to be vulnerable, humble, and transparent. They force us to find the good, make confessions, and voice our needs. The second question in particular is vital to us staying in the light as individuals and in our marriage.

I'm convinced that, if given the opportunity and a safe space, many of us would make confessions more often. Each week when my husband asks me if I've felt guilty or convicted of something, he allows me a chance to reflect honestly and bring anything that's buried back up to the surface. He affords me the possibility to nip sin in the bud and say aloud whatever is tempting me so that it cannot have power over me.

My answers to each of the three questions vastly vary, but occasionally they look like me admitting that I felt good when another guy complimented my appearance or me apologizing for being harsh when I could've been gentler. Every time I say the thing I wouldn't want someone to know about me out loud, its grip on me loosens, and I'm empowered.

Staying in the light is often awkward, but it's imperative to our inner health.

My Commitment to You

It might seem odd to write a commitment to thousands of strangers, but I feel it's an important step forward on my own personal path toward light, wholeness, and, ultimately, freedom.

And so, I vow to continue living in the light through the tending of my soul. I commit to living with integrity through a regular practice of confession. I promise not to teach what I have yet to practice. I pledge to live my life in pursuit of Jesus and wholeness.

I devote my writing career to creating a space where people can bring their full, true selves and find solidarity. I will continue telling the truth, because it's all we've got.

My Hope for You

I hope you will not spend your life striving for a smaller figure, a larger bank account, or more reasons to blame others for your struggles. I hope you will find peace in the body God gave you, joy in the ability to give generously, and freedom in the ownership of your soul. I hope you abandon a life of impressing to step into authentic living. That you choose radical honesty so you can really heal.

Pursue self-awareness so you can see yourself for who you really are and accept that person. Stop beating yourself up but don't settle for an unhealthy version of who God created you to be. Find the courage within yourself to believe that what God says about you is true: you are loved, you are whole, and you are worthy. Quit hiding and instead incorporate the practice of confession in your daily life. Stop suppressing things that feel hard and heavy. Confront your sin fearlessly, and deliberately choose grace. Refuse to hang your head in shame. Live loved and forgiven. Don't be embarrassed when you make mistakes or face rejection; keep putting yourself out there and gain confidence that only an identity rooted in God can explain. Be real in a world that lures you to fake it instead. Maintain integrity, for it is inescapable. Swap your self-consciousness for a beautiful soul-consciousness. Believe that you're already good. Live with purpose, not for performance. Celebrate every person you are tempted to compare yourself against. Give the benefit of the doubt to everyone you meet. Take ownership over your junk and quit blaming and justifying, which only prolong the inevitable. Count the fruit of your life and uproot anything that comes up rotten. Don't allow stagnancy to be an acceptable standard of living. Evolve. Be willing to do what it takes to get what you want most. Don't you dare play it small just to be liked. Stay hopeful. Find fulfillment in Jesus, rather than your accomplishments or relationships. Fight for an abundance mindset. Pace yourself. Acknowledge your limitations.

You have this one "wild and precious life" to live.[3] Will you care for your soul to make it count?

And let us consider how we may spur one another on toward love and good deeds, not giving up meeting together, as some are in the habit of doing, but encouraging one another—and all the more as you see the Day approaching. (Heb. 10:24–25)

SOUL CARE PRACTICE NO. 15
Stay in the light.

Be Radically Honest with Yourself

1. How do you protect your mental health?
2. What affirmation can you speak over yourself to rewrite a negative script?
3. Do you invite people into your struggles, and who is one person in your life who invites you into theirs?
4. What have you experienced that you can't keep to yourself, and why are you so passionate about it?
5. How will you proactively live in the light?

Acknowledgments

Ever since I can remember, I've been flipping to the back of books to read the acknowledgments first. This part reveals a lot about the author—who they love, appreciate, and were influenced by along the way. And so, these are the people who played a behind-the-scenes role in bringing this book to life.

E, my incredibly handsome, playful, and kind husband. Thank you for taking on the majority of parenting duties at various times so I could have solo weekends to write. For 11:00 p.m. runs to get me cookies and milk. For listening to me rehash concepts and stories one million times. Saying thank-you will never be enough. Your name deserves to be on the cover just as much as mine. You are the very best teammate, the Pippen to my Jordan. I love you!

Shia, my sweet son. Thank you for your bright-eyed, gummy smile whenever I walk through the door. For being my constant compass to God. You're only five months old today, but I need you to know that I welcome and love all of who you are becoming. Thank you for giving me yet another reason to choose integrity as we journey through the days ahead.

Bear, Skittles, and Goof, my beautiful, resilient, smart boys. Thank you for helping me experience the Spirit of God in new ways, believing that I'm the best author in the world, and helping me set my work aside to have fun. Being present with you has been some of my most important work.

Our many other little (and not so little) loves who have come and gone throughout our foster journey. You have made me become more self-aware. You have taught me to trust in Jesus when the stakes are high. You have allowed me to play a small part in your story. Thank you. You've played an even bigger role in mine. For you, I am always available.

Mama, thank you for teaching me that integrity is the most beautiful trait, leading by example, and being my biggest fan. You are a safe haven and a soft place to land. You are evidence of God's love for me. Thank you for raising me to believe I could do anything. I truly believe I am the luckiest person ever to have you as my mom and Mimi to all of my children. I hold you in high regard and still want to be just like you when I grow up.

Dad, thank you for owning your mistakes, which has ultimately taught me to own my own. I am so grateful we have experienced redemption in our relationship. It is proof that grace always wins. I know you love me and are proud of me. I hope you know that I also love you and am proud of how far you've come.

My entire Carpenter family, thank you for loving me not as an "in-law" but as your very own daughter and sister. Marrying into the family we have is a dream come true.

Rocio, my mentor turned soul-sister. Thank you for constantly encouraging me, holding up a mirror for me, and being the flesh of Jesus when I needed it most.

Katie, my mentor and cheerleader. Thank you for taking a chance on me, creating opportunities for me to grow as a communicator, and always caring about my heart more than the numbers.

Stephanie Smith, my editor. Thank you for helping me frame this book in a way that would best serve readers, embracing my messy first draft, and fighting for this book to get picked up the second time around. Your willingness to take a chance on me and your ability to see this book for what it could be has changed my life.

Tawny Johnson, my agent. Thank you and Illuminate Literary Agency for being on my team and guiding me every step of the way, especially when things took a weird turn in 2020. I have never felt alone in this, and I am forever thankful to be part of the Illuminate family.

Allie, my assistant turned dear friend. Working alongside you is a dream. Thank you for being a voice of reason when I have doubts, believing in my mission, and filtering through my thousand daily ideas to make the best come to life.

Karen, my counselor. Thank you for providing a safe space, investing in my marriage, and ushering me toward the light. My soul is well largely because of the work you do.

Neil, my business coach turned therapist, friend, marketing specialist, and more. When you facilitated my Life Plan, you changed my life. God continues to use you in my life both personally and professionally, and I cherish our time together. Thank you for being a safe male in my story. Your labor is not in vain and continues to have a ripple effect on generations to come.

Anjuli, my internet BFF turned real-life friend and daily "vox" of reason. Thank you for telling me to turn up the volume when I'd rather go mute and for going first on the weirdly scary journey of launching a book into the world. You are such a gift to me.

My incredible friends. You know who you are. There are too many of you to name. If you're reading this and you think, *Me?* the answer is yes, *you.* Thank you for being people I do not have to perform for, prove to, or filter with. Thank you for putting up with my nonstop chatter and outrageous ideas, and loving me all the more.

My Granny. Thank you for speaking life over me since I was born. I've never had to wonder how proud you are of me. I know Papaw is in heaven smiling and telling everyone about his Sunshine's new book.

My launch team. Thank you for never putting me on a pedestal where I don't belong, for believing there isn't a single person we wouldn't love if we knew their story, and for sharing this book with the world.

Jason Adam Miller, aka J. I'm so glad I gained you as a brother when I married E. Thank you for being genuinely curious about me and my book. When you open your mouth to speak, people listen, and for good reason. I am thankful for the pastor you are and the wisdom I've gleaned from our conversations.

Morgan Harper Nichols. Thank you for being real in the green room where we first met, for your radical honesty with the world, and for graciously accepting the invitation to write the foreword of my book.

Annie F. Downs. Thank you for telling me that it wasn't a matter of *if* it would happen but *when*. You are a generous friend. It is an honor to tell people you are just as wonderful offline as you are online.

My pastors: Kelly Skiles, Jeanne Stevens, and Jarrett Stevens. Your leadership, insight, and thoughtful feedback have cultivated deeper transformation in me. Your teachings have deepened my personal relationship with Jesus. The mission of Soul City Church continues to work on me. Thank you.

Every person (mostly strangers on the internet) who told me I gave language to their feelings and experiences over the last eight years that I've been writing publicly, thank you. You make me fall in love with writing even more. Thank you for helping me discover this gift over and over again.

Notes

Chapter 1 My Hidden Secret

1. Laura Kann et al., "Sexual Identity, Sex of Sexual Contacts, and Health-Risk Behaviors among Students in Grades 9–12: United States and Selected Sites, 2015," *Morbidity and Mortality Weekly Report Surveillance Summaries* 65, no. 9 (2016): 1–202.

Chapter 2 Coming Clean

1. "Maya Angelou Quotes," Goodreads, accessed January 18, 2022, https://www.goodreads.com/quotes/5934-i-ve-learned-that-people-will-forget-what-you-said-people.

2. Peter Scazzero, *The Emotionally Healthy Leader: How Transforming Your Inner Life Will Deeply Transform Your Church, Team, and the World* (Grand Rapids: Zondervan, 2015), 28.

3. APA Division 12, "PTSD Clinical Practice Guideline: How Do I Know If I Need Therapy?" American Psychological Association, July 31, 2017, https://www.apa.org/ptsd-guideline/patients-and-families/seeking-therapy.aspx.

4. "Flannery O'Connor Quotes," Goodreads, accessed January 18, 2022, https://www.goodreads.com/quotes/315733-i-write-because-i-don-t-know-what-i-think-until.

Chapter 4 The One Thing That Changes Everything

1. Jennifer Thompson-Cannino and Ronald Cotton with Erin Torneo, *Picking Cotton: Our Memoir of Injustice and Redemption* (New York: St. Martin's Press, 2009).

Chapter 5 You Are Not the Only One

1. Jamie Ivey, *If Only You Knew: My Unlikely, Unavoidable Story of Becoming Free* (Nashville: B&H, 2018), 134.

2. "Liz Bohannon - Speaking Highlights," YouTube video, 6:23, uploaded by BigSpeak Speakers Bureau, February 22, 2021, https://www.youtube.com/watch?v=ERcciLhNBPg.

Chapter 6 Impressing Is Exhausting

1. Brené Brown, *Daring Greatly* (New York: Avery, 2015), 42.
2. "The Enneagram Type Combinations," The Enneagram Institute, accessed December 14, 2021, https://www.enneagraminstitute.com/the-enneagram-type -combinations.

Chapter 9 All the Things We Cannot See

1. Bob Goff, Twitter post, @bobgoff, December 29, 2015, https://twitter.com /bobgoff/status/681858284815552513.
2. Carl Jung, *Aion: Researches into the Phenomenology of the Self* vol. 9, part 2, *Collected Works of C. G. Jung*, trans. Gerhard Adler and R. F. C. Hull (Princeton: Princeton University Press, 1953), 71.

Chapter 10 It's Not Them, It's You

1. For a good source of more information, visit @nowhitesaviors on Instagram, https://www.instagram.com/nowhitesaviors/.

Chapter 11 What Dreams Are Made Of

1. Bessel van der Kolk, *The Body Keeps the Score: Brain, Mind, and Body in the Healing of Trauma* (New York: Penguin Books, 2015).
2. "Abigail Van Buren Quotes," Goodreads, accessed January 19, 2022, https:// www.goodreads.com/quotes/1162961-if-you-want-your-children-to-turn-out -well-spend.

Chapter 12 The Question You Should Be Asking

1. Sharon Hodde Miller, *Nice: Why We Love to Be Liked and How God Calls Us to More* (Grand Rapids: Baker Books, 2019), 5.
2. Wayne W. Dyer, "Why the Inside Matters," *Wayne's Blog*, accessed December 14, 2021, https://www.drwaynedyer.com/blog/why-the-inside-matters/.

Chapter 14 Growth Doesn't Happen by Accident

1. Jarrett Stevens, public message at Soul City Church, Chicago, Illinois, August 19, 2018.

Chapter 15 Turn the Lights On

1. "Suicide Claims More Lives Than War, Murder, and Natural Disasters Combined," American Foundation for Suicide Prevention, accessed November 7, 2021, https://supporting.afsp.org/index.cfm?fuseaction=cms.page&id=1226 &eventID=5545.
2. Lisa Firestone, "Busting the Myths about Suicide," Psychalive, accessed December 14, 2021, https://www.psychalive.org/busting-the-myths-about-suicide/.
3. Mary Oliver, "The Summer Day," *House of Light* (Boston: Beacon, 1990), 60.

About the Author

Manda Carpenter is a writer, a speaker, and an advocate committed to helping women grow in their relationships with God, self, and others. She is a neighbor, question-asker, and cheerleader of the underdog. Manda and her husband, Eric, are foster parents and hosts of *A Longer Table* podcast. They live with their son, Shia, in Los Angeles, California. For more, check out @mandacarpenter on Instagram and www.mandacarpenter.com.

CONNECT WITH *Manda*

mandacarpenter.com

FOLLOW HER ON SOCIAL MEDIA

mandacarpenter   MandaSueCarp

Manda Carpenter   MandaSueCarpenter